TRAVEL
BALANCE

A Unique Health Guide
for Your Journey

John Ayo

LifeBalance
Dallas, Texas

Praise for John Ayo and
Travel Balance

"This book is a must for every traveler! I travel internationally quite often and there a so many tips in this book to keep you healthy during your trip. I believe in natural solutions and this guide provides a comprehensive approach to stay healthy naturally while traveling."

—Esther Ferre, IBM General Manager

"A key health prevention strategy is reducing stress, and you reduce stress by being prepared and arming yourself with tips and practical pointers on what to do before, during, and after your trip. With the diligence of an engineer, the expertise of a world traveler, the passion of a great teacher, and the knowledge of a naturopath, John gives you a step-by-step, readable, common sense, preventive and naturopathic health guide that you'll want to refer to and take on every trip."

—David Holland, MD

"I travel on over 100 flights a year. Frequent travelers need a system to ensure maximum personal productivity while on the road. Corporations want their employees healthy while they represent the company across the globe. It simply makes financial sense. John's natural approach is a system that works to keep the mind and body healthy and fresh while on the road."

—Bob Jones, Vice President, IBM Corporation

"John has combined his many years of challenging business travel with his extensive knowledge of health principles and practices in bringing this book together. Whether one travels constantly for business or just wants to feel their best on that special vacation, this book will have effective tips on how to feel great while doing it well!"

—Paul Collett, DC

"John is an intelligent and gifted individual when it comes to alternative healing. He has a heart of gold and will do anything in his power to help someone achieve their ultimate health and balance."

—Cheannié Marquis L.Ac, Dipl. O.M. (acupuncturist)

"When I met John I wondered what does an IBM tech guy know about healing, well quite a lot actually. Dr John's knowledge of natural healing techniques is outstanding. He is a true healer. You will feel comfortable knowing this book will provide the energy, space, and consciousness you require to stay healthy and balanced while you travel."

—Sue Hegel, DC

Cover and interior design by Brian Moreland
Edited by Brian Moreland

Image airplane © rebius - Fotolia.com
Image sky © Alekss - Fotolia.com
Image waterfall © pavel vashenkov - Fotolia.com
Clipart airplane mountain © patrimonio designs - Fotolia.com
All EFT, Jin Shin Jyutsu, and Heart Meridians illustrations of hands, face, and body illustrated by Duane Castañón (Fiverr username cgipixel) and licensed to John Ayo through Fiverr. com.

ISBN: 978-1-63452-162-8

For more information about this book:
www.JohnAyo.com

To all of my teachers:

I have been extremely blessed to have so many amazing teachers in my life, both living and passed. May their wisdom live on with me and through this book to help improve the lives of all people.

Tonya,
Thanks for all that
you do to make this
world a better place.

Enjoy your journey!
John

Acknowledgements

I would like to extend my heartfelt gratitude to my wife, Michelle, and our children, Anthony and Allison, for being a part of my life, and for being such amazing teachers for me.

I would also like to thank my many friends and colleagues who helped me to shape this book into a tool that can truly serve others – specifically: Valerie Copley (niece), Rod Bishop, Carolyn Trimmer, Magali Goirand, Pilar Angel, Eileen McDonald, Bethlyn Gerard, Amber Harris and Leslie Green.

A super thank you to my friend and ND colleague Danette Goodyear (my essential oils teacher) – you are an amazing person, teacher, healer, and friend.

Thanks to IBM for giving me the opportunity to travel the world and meet so many amazing people and for the many lessons I learned in my fantastic career there.

And, last but not least, to my friend and editor, Brian Moreland, for taking someone who knows nothing about books and guiding me down the path to completion.

About the Author

John Ayo is a classical naturopath and Certified Biofeedback Specialist (CBS) and has been researching mind/body/spirit topics since 1976. He worked in sales for IBM for 27 years, where the stress of Corporate America caused him to examine his priorities in life. He began having health issues around 1999 that could not be addressed by the traditional medical model of "fixing symptoms." This led him on an amazing journey back to health . . . and to his true passion.

He graduated *magna cum laude* from Texas A&M in Civil Engineering, where he went on to earn his MBA. This problem-solving background has played a huge part in John's passion for natural health, where he continues to spend many hours researching the cause of health issues. This quest led John to pursue a Doctorate in Naturopathy (ND), which he completed in 2006. Naturopathy is a field of holistic or natural health that seeks to understand the cause of imbalances in the body that lead to symptoms, and educate people on the principles and lifestyle changes they can make to correct these imbalances.

John earned his black belt in Aikido in 2011. Aikido is a Japanese martial art that is the study of energy in motion, and more importantly how we can achieve balance in our lives. His mission is to make a positive and meaningful difference in people's lives by sharing the information that he has researched on natural health solutions.

Disclaimer

Please note that Travel Balance reflects only the personal views and experience of the author. The ideas and suggestions are based on John's own experience. There may be some ideas in the book that may not agree with traditional allopathic medicine.

Note – Important: The information contained in this book is for educational purposes only. The medical conditions discussed should only be cared for under the direction of a physician. Proper care from a physician should not be avoided, delayed, or discarded when there is a reason to consult a physician. This book is not designed to diagnose, treat, or prescribe any disease. The author accepts no responsibility for such use. Conditions requiring proper medical attention should be referred to a physician.

Table of Contents

Introduction

This book is the natural intersection of two of the favorite things in my life – natural health and traveling. At the end of my IBM career, I had the good fortune to travel around the world for about eight years teaching sales classes. I had a friend who recently found out that she needed to go to Thailand for business. She asked me about my recommendations for this trip, and that (along with similar questions from other friends) prompted me to write this book. The recommendations and stories that you'll read are based on my experience, and I hope that they will help you to better enjoy your travel (whether it be for business or pleasure) and possibly consider working on other areas of health in your life after your trip. I will spend quite a bit of time talking about international travel in this book, but there are also plenty of helpful tips for domestic travel as well.

How many times have you heard people talk about getting sick while on the road? This book gives travelers some good insights on how to stay healthy and balanced once they leave their house. The information in this book is the result of my extensive business travel experience over 27 years at IBM coupled with knowledge from my background in holistic health. I approach the topic by focusing on natural/healthy choices that you can make while traveling. Therefore, all of my recommendations will be based on whole foods, herbs, essential oils, and other natural health remedies that will help the body to heal itself. You may choose to have some prescription and over-the-counter drugs on hand for emergencies, but this book is focused on natural health tips and remedies.

There is a wide spectrum of beliefs when it comes to health. I was raised with the mindset of parents from the early 1900s, where you just went to the doctor and did what they said whenever you were sick. If they said to take this pill or get this surgery, you just did it . . . no questions asked! I followed this belief throughout most of my life, but as you'll read below, I had some events that caused me to change. I now know that we are all responsible for our own health (not our doctor), and as such should consult with a team of professionals to assist us in our healing journey, if required. You have to do your own research and not just listen to what others say (including me). So, if you take nothing else away from this book, please take the time to do your homework and take responsibility for your own health (and that of your family).

Only we can heal ourselves. Our body is an amazing healing machine, but we have to give it what it needs. Some of the tools that I'm recommending will aid your body in this healing. If you regularly take prescription or over-the-counter medications, then some of these suggestions might sound strange to you. You might be wondering if something you can buy at a health food store can really be as effective as a prescription medication. Keep reading.

This book is meant to be a travel health guide you can refer to for a variety of natural health tips for staying healthy and balanced, as well as some unique remedies if you get sick while traveling. Use what you're willing to try and disregard the rest. I will talk about things on a spectrum from the casual health traveler to the extreme healthy person who will go to great lengths to ensure good health.

I am personally more of a 90/10 person when it comes to travel – I do my best to eat well 90% of the time, but also balance that with experiencing some of the culture (and food) of my destination. You don't want to eat things that you know will make you sick, but you also don't want to miss out on a local favorite because you are avoiding a certain type of food.

I will also be talking about some energetic recommendations that can assist your body to balance the onslaught of frequencies from things like radiation, WiFi, cell phones, or other EMFs (electromagnetic frequencies) that can compromise the body's ability to heal more quickly. More and more research is confirming that we are energy beings swimming in a sea of energy. If the energetics around us are not beneficial, then it will pull energy out of our bodies – the same energy that is required to help us heal. It is in our best interest to remediate the energetic imbalances in our environment to the best of our ability.

My Path to Becoming a Naturopath

I was a very successful sales rep for IBM for 20 years. One of the highlights of my career was leading the team that closed the largest software deal in the history of the industry (over $1 billion) back in 1997. This sales opportunity took more than a year and half of development, with lots of high level executive exposure, and needless to say, stress. We closed the deal and were rewarded with lots of recognition after the sale, but I just didn't feel fulfilled. I prayed daily, asking for guidance to show me my passion, and it wasn't long after that I received my answer. I got sick!

I could barely sleep at night, was in pain most of the time, and felt like I had the flu most of the day. I went to all sorts of medical doctors, who ran a wide array of tests on me – upper GI (Gastro Intestinal – i.e. digestive system), lower GI, gall bladder tests, lots of blood work, etc. They said that everything looked okay, and that my sickness was all in my head. Now we know that stress can wreak some major havoc on the body, but this had continued for several years. Our twins were born right around this time, so that also contributed a little extra stress. I also used to get five or six sinus infections a year to top it off. A friend recommended that I try some alternative or natural health options, but I was not all that receptive at first. But, since I wasn't making much progress through the Western medical path, I took it into consideration and began my research.

My engineering training, coupled with an MBA, kicked in and helped me to analyze a wide variety of information from the Internet and books. I went to several chiropractors who did "specialty work" (not just spinal alignment), and I began to learn from them. I tried a wide variety of modalities like acupuncture, structural integration, colonics, energy medicine, homeopathy, vitamin/herb supplements, chiropractic, nutrition . . . the list goes on. I befriended many of my new doctors (all alternative doctors), and they became my teachers.

I was still working in sales at IBM but met a man who had a TV show on natural health, so I took a leave of absence from IBM to work with him for a while. I had the opportunity to meet many of the guests on his show who were very knowledgeable and successful in the natural health area. This inspired me to pursue a path in natural health, so I enrolled in a doctorate program for naturopathy. I didn't know any traditional naturopaths at the time, but, after researching degrees, chose naturopathy because it was the most general and would help me get the broadest background possible in areas like acupuncture, homeopathy, herbology, iridology, nutrition, energy medicine, and many others. Our twins were very young, so I would study in the morning before they woke up, during nights and weekends, and during my flights for IBM business travel. It took me just over three years to earn this degree, called an ND (doctor of naturopathy). As naturopaths, we believe that the body will heal itself if we give it what it needs and remove the things that are causing it harm.

As I was studying and implementing these new ideas into my life, I began to feel better and better. As my health improved, the passion inside began to build and I wanted to share all of this new information with others. Early on my path, I worked with a nutritionist who introduced me to Juice Plus+ (a whole food supplement of fruits, vegetables, grapes and berries in a capsule), and I began to do presentations for my local team of representatives here in Dallas. I also discovered Young Living essential oils (our most ancient medicines) and added the incredible power of these tools into my life and work.

I knew that I had found my calling – to use my experience and talents to help make a positive and meaningful difference in people's lives. My prayers had been answered, but now the real work was just beginning.

Other Benefits from This Book

I moved into a sales training job in IBM in 1996 and started to teach a natural health section as an optional part of our class (at night). I was nervous to do a presentation on health for IBMers at my first class at the Xerox center outside of Washington

DC, and clearly remember that I had a terrible sinus infection at the time. The irony was staggering. But, I figured that if I could talk about health while clearly being sick, I could handle just about anything. I got great feedback from the students and began adding more life/work balance topics into my classes. This new job was the beginning of my international travel experience and allowed me to incorporate many of the new lessons I had learned while on the road.

I was now seeing a few clients on the side while teaching these classes and invested in an amazing computer system called the L.I.F.E. System that could help balance frequencies in the body using biofeedback. It was a perfect modality for me as it combined natural health with my technology background. I'll explain more about what biofeedback is and the amazing healing benefits you can get from it later in this book. After several years of working with clients, I earned my certification as a biofeedback specialist (requires 500+ hours of sessions) and continue to see clients. You can learn more about this at my website www.JohnAyo.com. I also continued my education by learning about several professional lines of supplements – Standard Process (SP) and Premier Research Labs (PRL) – both of which you'll see referred to in this book. Both of these companies provide outstanding education on how to best use whole food supplements to assist the body in its natural healing process.

Based on my experience, I will be giving you my specific recommendations for the products that I use when traveling. You are obviously free to use these specific products or choose to use something else, but as with most things in life, you get what you pay for, and as a result, you may not experience the results that I am describing. So, when I talk about certain products, you need to know that there are a wide variety of competitive offerings in the market with differing degrees of quality. I use these specific products (from vendors I recommend in this book) because I trust the quality of the products that they produce and am satisfied with the results that I see. Both Juice Plus+ (JP) and Young Living (YL) products are only sold by distributors and are not available in stores, so if you know someone who sells them, please get your products from them. If not, I offer websites[1] in the back of this book where you can order some of these products.

Standard Process products are only sold through medical doctors, chiropractors, naturopaths, acupuncturists, and other health professionals, so if your doctor or natural health care provider sells it, you can get the products from them. In addition to offering advice about keeping your body healthy and balanced, I'll be sharing some practical traveling tips that will help you be prepared before and during your travels, which should help to reduce stress.

I wish you only the best of health and beautiful experiences in your travels.

John Ayo

A link to a brief video introduction from John can be found at http://tinyurl.com/nwxcg43.

Abbreviations for Recommended Products

JP = Juice Plus+

PRL = Premier Research Labs

SP = Standard Process

YL = Young Living

Chapter 1

Pre-Trip Travel Fun:
What to Bring

Whether traveling for business or pleasure, I always look forward to preparing for a trip. Are you taking a vacation to Hawaii? A week-long cruise through the Caribbean? Touring Europe? Taking a business trip to Tokyo? Or perhaps just visiting family a few states away? Wherever you're going, there's something exciting about anticipating traveling to a destination, seeing new places, or visiting familiar ones. My goal is that you stay balanced and healthy, so your journey is a positive experience full of great memories.

A big part of staying healthy begins with the preparation of what to bring with you, balanced with packing just the right amount of stuff. I have included quite a bit of information on preparing for your trip (including a detailed checklist) with the hope that you won't need to use most of it. So as I list all the things that I bring, keep in mind that I like to be prepared for every scenario, from eating the healthiest foods to having natural remedies on hand when I feel unbalanced or an illness coming on. As we often say in IBM – "expect the best, and prepare for the worst." So when packing for your trip, take only the things you feel you need most.

Pre-Trip Health

Supplements

These are the products that I use and recommend. It's up to you whether you choose to use these specific products or something else. In general, I believe that if we give our bodies good food (think organic fruits and vegetables) and clean water, then we really don't need a lot of supplements. But, given the challenge in eating (especially when traveling), the extra stress and the toxic state of our planet today, I think it's a good idea to add a few supplements to your travel list.

> **To maintain good health and wellness, it's important to develop a preventive mindset.**

One of the most important concepts that you'll hear me talk about throughout this book is the idea that in order for natural health products/supplements to work, you have to come from a preventive mindset. If you wait until you're already sick to start doing something about it, you may not experience the positive results that you would like to achieve. Along those lines, it's important that you begin taking extra supplements one or two weeks before your trip (depending on where you are going and how long you'll be gone). If you are traveling to a location that has known travel health issues, like India or Mexico, you'll want to begin several weeks prior.

I take a little extra JP Fruits, Veggies, and Vineyard blend and YL Life 5 probiotics about a week prior to my departure date. This helps my body to build up additional immunity and seed the digestive system with beneficial bacteria. I also recommend the SP ProSynbiotic and PRL Probiotic Caps as alternative probiotic supplements. Each supplement may come with different directions in terms of how best to take them. Some products will advise you to take them on an empty stomach (at least thirty minutes before food, or two hours after eating), while others advise to take with food.

Diet

It would be best to clean up your diet a week or so before your trip. There are many books written on diet and nutrition (see www.JohnAyo.com/Favorites), so I won't go into too much detail here. I'm a pretty big fan of a Mediterranean Diet, but am okay with most diets that include as many fruits and vegetables as possible. In my experience, eating sugar, dairy, and wheat are well known ways to weaken your immune system. I've heard that drinking half of a sugar soda can deplete your immune system by 50% for up to eight hours. Since we want a super robust immune system, we'll want to avoid these types of foods and drinks as much as possible, especially before a long trip.

Packing Checklist

One of *the* most beneficial tools to help avoid the stress associated with packing (with somewhat regular travel) is a packing checklist. You can save yourself an incredible amount of time and worry by building and maintaining this list. I would recommend that you build it in a word processing document (vs. writing it on paper), as it's much easier to edit. You can search for one of the many mobile apps (for example, EverNote) available in the app market as well, as they help to keep things synced between multiple electronic devices. With EverNote, for example, you can update your packing list while you're on the trip (of course, you can do this with the word processing document as well, but that would require your computer), and it will sync to all of your devices (e.g. computer, phone, tablet, etc.). I use a Word document with checkbox bullets so that I can print it and easily check things off as I prepare them for packing. Here is a sample from my packing list (more detailed list in the Appendix):

- ☐ Essential Oils

  - ○ Thieves hand cleaner, oil and spray

  - ○ Valor, Peace and Calming, ImmuPower, Lemon, Peppermint, StressAway, DiGize, White Angelica, Gratitude

  - ○ Travel diffuser (plug in) or cotton balls

  - ○ Lip balm

- ☐ Food

  - ○ Snacks/trail mix/energy bars

I spend a large amount of my time packing all of my "just in case" items. Many of the items I'm packing (especially if going on a long trip) will never be used, but it's sure nice to have them if you need them. Examples of this are supplements specifically for food poisoning, which I hope to never have . . . but nice to have if you run into this. I typically pack items that I use every day while at home, but for these "just in case" items, I store them in a special bag that I just put in my checked luggage. That way, I won't have to continue to pack and unpack them. They are already in their emergency kit. Similarly, I keep a quart size plastic bag handy for my carry-on liquid items, so that I can just throw this into my carry-on bag (e.g. items like small toothpaste, lip balm, eye drops, etc.). I use a pill box that has compartments for supplements for seven days (two compartments per day), so I will fill this box up with supplements to reduce the number of bottles that I need to carry. If my trip is longer than a week, then I'll pack the replacements in as few bottles as possible. If you use one of these pill boxes, be sure to wrap it in plastic wrap before packing. I learned from experience that when bags get jostled (as they often do when traveling), the pills that were inside the container don't stay there very long. This is not the best surprise when you begin unpacking at your destination, as you have to try to figure out which pills go on which days – without their bottles! Even worse, if the capsules break open you will get a nice dusting on your clothes with herbal powders.

If my departure time is early in the morning, I will pack the night before, otherwise, I like to pack on the morning of the trip (if afternoon departure). This way I have already used all of my morning items and can then pack them directly. I like to go through the checklist and put all of the items on my bed. Once I have them all on the bed, I will put them into either the checked bag (or overhead bag) or my carry-on bag.

Don't forget to add electrical chargers to your list. You don't want to get all prepared to watch that movie you downloaded onto your tablet only to find that you have no battery power. They now have external battery chargers that you can bring with you to charge your electrical devices. If you are on a long flight, you should choose a seat with a power outlet (you'll notice a little lightning bolt next to the seat number under the overhead bin). You can use a seat selection tool on the Internet (e.g. seatguru.com) to help you choose a seat with an outlet. Note that some planes have DC outlets (like the ones you'd use to charge something in your car – i.e. car adapter), and some of the newer planes have AC outlets (like you use at home). I know I've sat on a few flights where the outlet was behind me, and I had to ask the people sitting there if they minded me plugging in my cord from my seat. It's usually fine with people . . . until they have to go the lavatory and forget it's there.

Pre-Trip Shopping

While it's great to be able to just pull things out of the closet or cabinet as you go through your checklist, you may need to do a little shopping to get some of the consumables for your trip. Since you never know when you may be stuck somewhere with no healthy food choices, it's a good idea to pack some of your own. Here are a few items that I recommend:

- Instant oatmeal

- Dried/packaged soup

- Tea bags

- Bars

- Trail mix

- Fruits and veggies

- Laundry from cleaners

• **Low Sugar Instant Oatmeal** – You'll see a theme here for items that only require hot water to make. There have been many trips where I've had a flight at 6:00 AM and have to get up before 4:00 AM to get a taxi to the airport. It's times like these that I am thankful to have some instant food in my suitcase. I've found that most hotels around the world have an electric kettle in the room, which I can use to boil water. If not, I use the coffee maker. If I don't have either in my room, I will call the front desk and see if they can help. I always use bottled water to make the oatmeal. Remember to pack some utensils as well. I did not pack any once and had to eat my oatmeal with plastic stir sticks from the hotel room (at 3:30 AM). Look for instant oatmeal with less than 6 grams of sugar – no sugar is best.

• **Dried/packaged soup** – It's best to get the envelopes of soup at the store (rather than the Styrofoam cups – which may get crushed in your luggage and are actually toxic to our bodies). Try to find soup mixes that have the least amount of ingredients possible, as they are more likely to be the healthy ones. I opt for the more healthy brands that you would buy at a health food store, even if I have to pay a little bit more for them.

• **Tea bags** – If you are a tea drinker, it's a good idea to bring some of your favorite tea along to use on your trip.

- **Bars** – These are arguably one of the most convenient foods that you can travel with, as they are self-contained. The main things that I look for when I purchase nutrition bars are:

  ○ Ingredients – whole foods, herbs or spices I recognize (vs. synthetic chemicals) – when you read ingredient labels, the list is sorted by amount, so the items at the beginning of the list have the biggest quantity. Sugar – <10g is preferable – less is better – be sure to look at the ingredient list for other names of sugar, like high fructose corn syrup or dextrose, and avoid those products. Less sugar is best, but artificial sugars can be the worst. Fiber – 3g+ – the more fiber the better

  ○ Protein (10-15g)

  ○ No trans fats or partially hydrogenated oils

  ○ Low glycemic index – to keep blood sugar more stable

  ○ Omega 3 essential fatty acids (e.g. flax seeds)

  ○ Gluten/dairy free is a positive, as is vegan.

An added bonus is if you like the taste. However, I've come to a point in my health journey that if a bar has a good nutrition profile at a reasonable price, I can learn to like the taste of it.

I like the JP Complete bars, as they have a healthy combination of ingredients and taste good. Young Living has several bars in their catalog that are very nutritious and I like as well. Take a look at the ingredients in your favorite bar to make sure that it isn't more candy bar than health bar.

- **Trail mix** – There is a variety of trail mix that you can buy or make. You can even get some at most airports, but I can create my own mix that is better from a cost and quality perspective. I like to go to my favorite local health food store and buy some trail mix in bulk. Then I put it in plastic bags (sandwich or quart size, depending on the length of the trip) and take it with me. I have to tell you that on one trip to New Zealand, I made sure that I filled up a quart bag so that I wouldn't be hungry on the plane – and beyond. I got lucky on this trip and was upgraded to business class, so didn't need to eat any of my stash on the flight over. I thought that was great as I'd have more to eat for the rest of my week. But, when I got to the airport, I found out that you couldn't bring nuts and seeds into the country, so was forced to throw away the whole bag!

The selection process for trail mix is similar to that of the bars. Get something that isn't a big bag of sugar disguised as trail mix. Examine the ingredients as you would energy bars, looking at grams of sugar, high fructose corn syrup, and dextrose. The good thing about trail mix and health bars is that you can eat them for several weeks as they are sealed, self-contained food that travels and is well preserved – very handy. One note of caution: peanuts[1] are really legumes and research has shown that they tend to be contaminated with aflatoxin (type of fungus), so are best to avoid.

- **Fruits/Vegetables** – On the other side of the spectrum of longevity (how long the food stays preserved) are fruits and vegetables. These are a wonderful thing to bring with you, but won't last very long. You can cut up some fruits and vegetables in a plastic bag to bring on the plane, but know that they will be going through the X-Ray machine at the airport.

Consider shopping ahead for food to eat at your destination, especially for a domestic trip. I have a friend that packs a box of food – protein powder, greens powder, other nutritional supplements, and a mixer and ships it to her destination hotel a few days before her arrival. This way, she has everything she needs to prepare healthy meals in her hotel room. I have not personally done this, but I think it's a good idea, if you know you'll be eating in the room most of the time. You can also pack a box of food to check as baggage on your flight.

• **Laundry** – If you are packing any clothes that you'd get from the professional cleaners, ask them to fold the clothes for you. I do this for my button-down shirts. These pack much more easily. It's a good idea to take the clothes that you get from the cleaners out of the plastic bag and let them air out (preferably outside) before packing them, so that the residue from any cleaning solutions that are used are not concentrated in your luggage right next to your other packed items.

What to Take on the Plane

Now we're getting to one of the tricky parts of travel – how to balance what you can bring on the plane with what you really need. This area tends to be subjective, so I'm passing on my time-proven suggestions. In general, you'll want to have some "just in case" items, entertainment, and food. The length of the flight will determine how much you'll want to bring, so for discussion purposes, I'm going to assume a 17-hour flight . . . in coach (worst case)!

• **Food** – I recommend that you complete a traveler profile with your airline. If you use a regular travel agent, you can also do this with them. There are food profile options (e.g. vegetarian, Kosher, etc.) that you can choose from that will automatically track back to your flight as a "special meal." If you don't do this, you are subject to the "meal of the day," which varies quite a bit depending on the airline and flight.

> **Water is your best friend**
>
> **on an airplane.**

• **Drinks** – Being on a plane is extremely dehydrating for your body due to the dry air (as the air at higher altitudes has very low humidity), so you will want to drink as much filtered water as you possibly can. You can either buy a big bottled water after you've cleared through security (which I *highly* recommend), or bring an empty bottle and ask the flight attendant to fill it up for you. While this may seem like a simple request, keep in mind that many flight attendants may not have the time or desire to do this for you and will say that they can only give you a plastic cup with water. It helps to be kind to people – and these folks need all the kindness they can get. If you ask nicely, they may fill your bottle for you. Otherwise, just ask for 2 cups of water with no ice. Be sure that they fill your bottle with *only* filtered water. If they are pouring from a plastic bottle, then it's "probably" filtered, but the only way to make sure is to ask. If they only have a metal pitcher with water in it, then the water is most likely not filtered. If you run into this situation, then the next best option is club soda, which should come from a can and have filtered water with carbonation. Take a look at the list of available beverages in the back of the airplane magazine and determine your best options before the flight attendants get to your seat, in case they don't have filtered water available. I have not personally run into a situation where they did not have filtered water, as they are usually very prepared. I try to drink about 8 oz. of filtered water per hour of flight.

While it would be great to bring your own tea bags to use on the plane, the challenge is getting filtered hot water. The flight attendants can give you hot water, but from what I've heard (from my flight attendant friends), this is not the best idea. The water they use for coffee/tea is not from bottles, and is not filtered, so I would avoid coffee and tea. It is a good idea to bring some tea bags for when you get to your hotel room, as you can use filtered water there.

• **Clothes** – The temperature in an airplane can vary quite a bit, so it's a good idea to bring/wear layers of clothes. I remember a flight recently where it was really cold, and when I asked for a blanket was told that it would cost $4! That's an interesting revenue generating idea – crank up the A/C and charge for blankets (not that they would do that).

When I have had the good fortune to travel in business class, most airlines gave me a goody bag with some items in it – one of which is a pair of socks. Now, these are not the best socks in the world, but they can come in handy when you are flying. So, if you're not traveling in business or first class, you might consider bringing a pair of socks with you. I would also recommend that you bring a light jacket or fleece pullover as well.

If you have checked your luggage, and your trip involves multiple connections, you will definitely want to pack a change of clothes in your carry-on bag. From a planning perspective, I assume that I won't see my checked bag on the other end, even though I expect to. "Expect the best and plan for the worst" is a good packing/travel motto to follow. You can always go shopping at your destination, but at least bring enough to last a day or so.

• **Airplane bag** – I've seen many travelers with small bags on the plane to carry most of their "essentials." I usually don't use this, but thought I'd mention it here, as it can be a good idea. If you travel a lot, it's nice to just pick up this one bag that has all of your small items in it. Some things to consider putting in the bag are tissues, ear plugs, hair bands, a small toothbrush and toothpaste, eye glasses (if you wear contacts), hand cream, lip balm, and eye drops. It is nice to have some moisturizing cream that can help with chapped lips and dry hands/feet (due to the dry air). I usually bring a bottle of basic lubricant eye drops, especially for long flights. Remember, if you use this small bag approach, you'll still need to put the creams and drops in the plastic bag to check through security. That is one of the other reasons why I keep my liquids in the plastic bag and put that bag in the seat pocket in front of me upon boarding. Funny story, at the airport in Colombia, they have security officers with dogs that walk around smelling luggage. I was standing by the luggage carousel waiting to retrieve my luggage when one of them came to visit me. The security guard asked me some questions – in Spanish (which I didn't completely understand as I am not fluent) – while the dog was sniffing my backpack. After a few minutes I realized what the dog was smelling – my plastic bag with essential oils!

• **Essential Oils** – My travel oils take up a large portion of my quart-size, plastic bag, and are definitely on the "must have" list when I get on a plane. The versatility of the oils is what makes them such great travel companions. I use only therapeutic grade (highest quality) oils from Young Living. Here is how I use them:

- **Internally** – It is possible to ingest some of the therapeutic grade oils to aid the body in healing. Check with essential oil information guides that are on the market to see which oils and blends are safe to ingest (I use the *Essential Oil Desk Reference* from lifesciencepublishers.com[2]). For example, the two main oil blends that I ingest quite often when traveling are Thieves (for helping my body fight off infection) and DiGize (for digestive issues).

- **Topically** – Apply certain oils to the skin directly for particular issues (some require that you dilute them in a carrier oil like almond or sesame oil). For example, if you are experiencing pain, you might use a YL oil blend called Deep Relief. It comes in a roll-on applicator and you apply it directly to the area that is in pain. One precaution is that you should not apply oils in the eyes or ears. It's okay to apply around those areas as directed by essential oil reference guides and may require dilution. If you need to dilute the oils after application, do not use water, as it will not work! You must use a vegetable or nut oil (I like sesame oil) to dilute the oils, so it's a good idea to pack a small bottle of carrier oil for this reason.

○ **Inhale** – I like to take the lid off of a bottle and inhale directly from the bottle, or place a few drops in my palm, rub my palms together and cup over my nose to inhale. Put a few drops of a single oil or blend on a cotton ball or tissue and put that in a plastic bag. Then open the bag to inhale the oil on the plane. Purchase an aromatic pendant or small container that is used to hold the oils for inhalation. Many oils can quickly impact the limbic system of the brain (center of emotions), helping to create a calming (or other type) effect. They are very powerful.

Diffusers get the oils into the air, but you won't be able to use a diffuser on the plane. You can pack a diffuser and use it in your hotel room or destination office, as long as you have a compatible electrical adapter.

The following list is not meant to be complete or required, but, here are a few oils that I like to use when traveling. Please don't think that you have to have *all* of these – just choose a few that resonate with you to begin.

> ## YL Thieves® essential oil is a #1 must have for travelers.

○ **Thieves** – Helps boost the immune system to fight off all infections. You can put a few drops (I use 5) in a capsule and take twice a day for prevention or if feeling sick. Apply to the bottom of the feet twice per day. Put a few drops in water and drink it, or just put a few drops in your mouth if you feel like you're getting sick. You can also diffuse it in the hotel room to get rid of smells and sanitize the room.

○ **Valor** – Courage, helps with traveling around lots of people. Apply to bottom of feet before traveling. Might also apply to back of neck and wrists. Great to use daily, as it helps your body to stay in alignment, which is helpful when your chiropractor is not along with you on your trip.

○ **Peace and Calming** – Apply to bottom of feet, temples, and wrists. Rub palms and inhale.

- **ImmuPower** – Applied to bottom of feet daily. Will strengthen the immune system to fight off any infections preventively.

- **Lemon, Grapefruit, Citrus Fresh, Orange, Tangerine, Lime** – Citrus oils are great to smell and add to water. If you are adding to water, make sure it's a glass container and not a plastic or Styrofoam cup (it will eat through these and break down the chemicals from the plastic or Styrofoam into the water). I mostly use these after arriving at my destination, or you can put a few drops on your tongue and then drink some water on the plane.

- **Peppermint** – Digestion, sinus, nausea and headache relief. Can also help with alertness (if you want to stay awake). Rub palms and inhale. Apply to feet, temples, and wrists. You can also add to your water, as with the citrus oils above.

- **StressAway** – Rub palms and inhale, or inhale directly from the bottle.

- **DiGize** – Digestion, nausea, parasites, food poisoning – can apply on the stomach or the bottom of the feet directly, or take internally. I usually put 2-3 drops in a small cup with water and drink.

- **White Angelica** – Helps with general protection when around lots of people (e.g. picking up other people's "stuff") and radiation. This is very helpful for those who are more sensitive.

- **Gratitude** – Inhale as needed. Smells good and just reminds me to stay in a state of gratitude.

- **Ginger** – Great for nausea, digestive issues, and motion sickness. You can apply to the wrists, palms, and/or just inhale.

- **Lavender** – Most universal of all oils. Helps to keep you calm. Apply to bottom of feet, temples, and wrists. Put a few drops in your palms, rub in a circle, and inhale.

- **Thieves hand cleaner, spray, and wipes** – I use one or two pumps of the spray in my mouth if I feel any type of scratchy throat on the plane. You can also use the spray or wipes to sanitize the area around you – tray table, video remote, etc.

- **Bon Voyage Travel Pack** – contains 10 YL personal-care products inside an attractive, custom-designed bag:

1. Cinnamint Lip Balm

2. Genesis Lotion

3. Lavender Conditioner, 2 oz.

4. Lavender Shampoo, 2 oz.

5. Morning Start Bath & Body Gel, 2 oz.

6. Thieves Dental Floss

7. Thieves Mouthwash, 2 oz.

8. Thieves Waterless Hand Purifier, 1 oz.

9. Thieves Aromabright, 2 oz.

10. YL toothbrush

There are many books that discuss in detail how to best use essential oils, and I would encourage you to explore this topic further. I highly recommend the *Essential Oil Desk Reference* book.

• **Supplements** - I like to have certain supplements on hand for those "just in case" moments on an airplane. Here are a few that I like to bring with me on the plane (again, don't feel like you need to have ALL of these right away):

  ○ **Inner Defense** – This Young Living product is basically the Thieves blend with a few added oils (i.e. oregano and thyme) in a capsule form. I will take one twice a day if I feel the slightest inkling of anything funny going on in my body.

○ **Colloidal Silver** – Many people use this on a regular basis to help boost their immune system. Some people think of it more as a last resort in fighting off infection, when in reality it should be more of a first choice. It is a natural antimicrobial and will help the body to naturally remove pathogens such as bacteria, viruses, yeast, candida, fungus, and some parasites. I have used it in the past to help with eye irritations, as I will put a drop in my eyes to help fight off infection. You can also pour it into a cut to disinfect the area.

○ **PRL Green Tea ND** – This is a product I like to take while in the air.

○ **No Jet Lag** – Homeopathic remedy that I use when traveling internationally[3].

○ **Daily supplements** – I like to put at least two days' worth of these into a plastic bag to bring on the plane (so that I can take them throughout the flight) and pack the seven-day container in my carry-on bag. This way, you will have your key supplements with you if your bags don't arrive with you at your destination. If you normally take Juice Plus at home, you will want to have your Fruits, Veggies, and Vineyard with you on the plane.

○ **Digestive support** – I like to bring digestive enzymes like YL Essentialzyme or Essentialzymes-4, SP Enzycore, PRL Digest. and also PRL Betaine HCL supplements with me as these can help support digestion when eating food from the airline. Depending on the situation, you may or may not want to eat the food served to you. I have been on some flights (especially in Asia), where it's hard to recognize what you are being served. This is where the bars come in handy! But, if you do decide to eat the airplane food, it's a good idea to take some digestive enzymes along with your meal, as they can help your body to digest your meal. You can use many types of digestive enzymes and Betaine HCL, as well as the DiGize oil blend or Peppermint oil to help support your body's digestion.

Summary

○ To maintain good health and wellness, it's important to develop a preventive mindset

○ Create/edit your packing checklist

○ Go shopping early for items that you'll need when packing, especially if you are order-ing from a distributor or on the Internet

○ Essential oils are great to take with you for a variety of health benefits, and Thieves is the number one to take

○ Water is your best friend on an airplane

Chapter 2

Plan Ahead to Reduce Stress

Organization

I like to keep the stress down before a business trip. To do this, I make sure I'm organized and have a working cell phone for international calling, any necessary paperwork, and my passport and/or visa current. If traveling to a foreign country, I'll exchange currency with a travel agent before I depart. Then I'll go through my pre-travel checklist the day before. Being organized assures that I will be stress-free when it's time to go on my trip.

Family Expectations

Depending on the length of your trip, you may want to have a chat with your family (spouse, kids, parent, etc.) about how often you plan to call home. While you are out exploring the world, they are all at home in their daily routines worrying (maybe) about you. So, you'll want to make sure that everyone is in agreement on a plan. It's a good idea to pick a specific time and do the best that you can to call at that time. Large differences in time zones will be a big factor here, along with the uncertainty of events on the road, so that's why planning ahead is important.

It is also a good idea to implement some "worry guidelines" – for example: "If you don't hear from me in XX days, then please call or email my manager at this number."

Airplane Seat Location

Seat preference is really up to you, but I like to sit near the front of the plane as much as possible. As you might suspect, there is quite a bit of radiation exposure in an airplane as we are closer to the sun for an extended period of time. There's not much you can do about the altitude, but if you are on a long flight, I would recommend that you try to reserve a seat on the side opposite from the sun for the majority of that flight. For example, if you are flying from Dallas to New York in the morning, the sun would be on your right (East) for most of the flight, so it might be best to reserve a seat on the left side of the plane (especially if you like window seats).

We know from quite a bit of research that green tea helps to protect our body from radiation. You could drink green tea on the flights (if you bring your own), but unfortunately the hot water on most flights is not filtered and you may be doing more harm than good. One particular supplement that I recommend is called Green Tea ND from PRL. It is a concentrated green tea liquid extract that contains nanized (extremely small particles) green tea phytonutrients and polyphenols. You simply add a few drops (up to several teaspoons) in your water and drink it during the flight. The longer the flight, the more I like to consume for protection.

Pack and Check (for longer or international flights)

- Food/Supplements – I pack my stash of bars and other food identified in the shopping section of this book along with my main supply of supplements in my checked bag (for longer trips). Here are a few supplement items that I like to pack and check:

  o YL NingXia Red packets – NingXia Red is a powerful antioxidant drink that contains whole NingXia wolfberry puree, a blend of blueberry, aronia, cherry, pomegranate, and plum juices, natural stevia extract, grape seed extract, pure vanilla extract, and orange, yuzu, lemon, and tangerine essential oils. I take this regularly at home and also bring packets when I travel.

○ SP St John's Wort – Can be used to help with jet lag or anxiety.

○ Probiotics – I use SP Prosynbiotic, PRL Probiotic Caps, and YL Life 5 – excellent to have on hand when traveling to make sure you keep your gut healthy, happy, and regular.

○ Omega 3 capsules – I use both SP Tuna or Cod Liver Oil, or YL OmegaGize. Essential fatty acids are foundational for health, as we can only get them from food. If you are traveling to a destination where you'll be eating lots of fresh seafood, you might not need to bring these.

○ YL Purification Oil – Good to have on hand for mosquito bites and insect repellant. I make my own spray by filling a small spray bottle with purified water and adding about 10 drops of YL Purification oil.

○ Melatonin – I use PRL Melatonin. It was the

first plant-based melatonin and is extremely pure. It's great to help you sync into a new time zone. I will talk more about how to use this in the chapter on jet lag.

○ Allergy support – PRL Allercaps (or SP Allerplex) and Vitamin C are great to have if you are known to experience inhalant allergy issues. The Allercaps can be taken to help with symptoms, and the whole food Vitamin C is beneficial to support the body with allergic reactions. The YL Super C Chewables are quite handy. I also bring SP Antronex – which is a natural antihistamine. I usually just have a handful of each of these in a small marked plastic bag, as I try not to carry too many supplement bottles.

If you use a neti pot on a regular basis at home, it's something you won't want to be without when traveling. The neti pot allows you to "rinse" your sinuses with warm water and salt. This helps to clear the sinus passages from a variety of inhalant particles. I have a plastic version of one that I bring with me, and I will use it throughout the trip as needed, especially upon arrival in my hotel room. Make sure to use filtered water that you have heated in your electric kettle or coffee maker, along with good quality sea salt that you bring from home. I like the ones that use Celtic, Himalayan, or Hawaiian sea salts, and personally use the PRL Pink Salt more than anything else.

○ Immune Support

☐ **SP Gastrex** – This is a must-have, "just in case" supplement as it will help your body with any type of food poisoning issues.

☐ **SP Immuplex** – This immune support product is good to take preventively to help your body fight off any infections. I usually take one capsule twice a day before, during, and after my trip.

☐ **YL ImmuPro** – This supplement contains a variety of immune boosting herbs along with melatonin and is good for nighttime use.

• Travel soap/shampoo – I know that the free shampoo, conditioner, and soap are appealing, but it's a good idea to bring your own quality (and toxin-free) products from home. The skin is the largest organ in the body and absorbs whatever we put on it. Make sure that the ingredients in the soap and shampoo that you use is all natural and free from harmful chemicals. I use many of the YL (and PRL) products here along with their toothpaste and deodorant.

Gary Young's (the founder of Young Living and fellow naturopath) philosophy is that any product you put on your skin should be clean enough to eat. They create their products with this level of purity.

- PRL Pyrafire Pyramid – Covered in the hotel room chapter.

- Tennis or golf balls – Great to have in your room so that you can roll your feet or other body parts on to help relieve muscle tightness.

- Umbrella – Good idea to pack a small travel size umbrella. You just never know.

- Universal electric adapter – You can bring the single kind, or the universal ones that have a bunch of different adapters in one. Since you sometimes don't know what type of plug you'll encounter, it's a good idea to get the universal one.

- Baseball cap or visor – It's a good idea to bring a hat of some kind, as you never know when you'll go exploring and need some sun protection.

- Sunscreen – If you are going to a place where you think you'll be in the sun, you should bring some good quality (non-toxic) sunscreen. I recommend researching your product at ewg.org (Environmental

Working Group), as they publish an annual report on non-toxic sunscreens. Remember that anything we put on our skin gets absorbed into the body.

• Passport – You will want to take extra good care of your passport if you are on an international trip. I keep my passport in my front pocket on the flight just to avoid any stress or possibility of having it fall out of my bag.

• Bring your *Travel Balance* book as a reference guide.

Summary

○ Do as many organizational things as you can before your trip to reduce stress

○ Establish a family communications schedule and expectations

○ Get some of the local currency before you go

○ Begin to support your immune system a week or two before your departure

○ Avoid sugar, dairy, and wheat before and during your trip (and hopefully most of the rest of your life too!)

○ Minimize the impact of radiation on your body by seat location and taking green tea extract supplementation

- Get clothes that you need to and from the cleaners

- Order supplements, sunscreen, or other items that you can't get locally

- Purchase a universal electric adapter if traveling internationally

- Remember your passport

Chapter 3

At the Airport

Security

Before we can thrive on the airplane, we have to make it to the plane, which means getting through security. From a health perspective, you need to be careful about the radiation that you are likely to encounter in security. There is a lot of debate about this topic (same with cell phone use). I tend to take the conservative side and assume that the radiation that we are exposed to in security, that is supposed to be "safe" for us, is not so safe – especially if you are a frequent traveler. I know that this area of protecting against something we can't see, and that society says is safe, might be difficult for some of you, but please approach it with an open mind. The electromagnetic spectrum is wide, with only a tiny portion that is visible to the human eye.

> **Our bodies are electrical and full of energy.**

Some of this electrical energy is easily visible with medical scans like EKGs (heart rhythms) and EEGs (brain waves) that measure the electrical impulses from the nervous system of the body. We also have a fiber optic light system that flows through the meridians of the body that acupuncturists work with to help our bodies heal. As energy beings, we are susceptible to outside EMFs (electromagnetic frequencies). Based on my 15 years of study in this area, I believe that these EMFs can interfere with the cell-to-cell communication inside of our bodies and cause harm to our immune system, among other things. It is in our best interest to minimize EMFs like the radiation of X-rays and scans as much as possible.

There are certain stones that can help to absorb this radiation. One of these is called tektite or moldavite. I carry one small piece of tektite in each pocket as I go through the older, low-radiation scanners (the kind where you simply walk through). If you get a TSA PreCheck authorization (in the U.S.), you can usually go through these older scanners at the airport. If that's the case, the tektite will be helpful in reducing the radiation exposure as you walk through, as it is believed to absorb some of the EMFs. There are also EMF protective necklaces that you can wear as well. If you do not have this approval, and are required to go through the newer devices (where you stand and place your hands over your head), you might consider opting out. As a frequent flyer, I always choose this route. You simply tell a security person that you'd like to "opt out" when you get to the front of the security line, and they will pull you aside and do a manual security check.

There may be no danger from these devices, but I'm not convinced that we really know enough yet to measure it, so would rather be conservative. It might take a little longer, and people may stare at you, but you have to decide for yourself if it is worth the extra effort.

If you are a U.S. Citizen and you travel internationally from time to time, I recommend that you look into the U.S Global Entry Program. This allows you to enter the U.S. through a passport kiosk and save time on your arrival back home. It costs about $100 (one time charge), but can be well worth it in terms of time savings. You may want to apply for the TSA PreCheck Program as well, as this will save you some time in getting through the security checkpoints in the U.S.

Once I've crossed the security checkpoint, I purchase a large bottled water. I prefer spring water if I can get it, but many times I don't have an option and can only get RO (reverse osmosis) filtered water, which is fine. Spring water tends to have more natural minerals than RO filtered water, which is why I prefer spring water, if I can get it. I don't drink out of the airport drinking fountains as that water is typically not filtered. It's worth noting that on some flights you may be forced to give up your water bottle (due to airport security) before boarding the plane. I'm not sure why this is, but it does happen occasionally in some airports. Also, you may be forced to leave security at certain airports in order to make a connecting flight. If that's the case, you will not be able to bring your full water bottle with you. I recently completed a trip to Colombia where I had to make a connecting flight in Miami. I was surprised that I had to leave the secure area to go to the gate for my connecting flight. When I entered the security checkpoint, I was reminded about my full water bottle and had to drink the whole thing before proceeding.

Airport Exercise

Once I have made it through security and purchased my water, I like to get in some pre-trip exercise. My first destination is to my gate to make sure that there are no surprises (and to make sure I know where the gate is). After that I start walking from one end of the airport to the other, and back until it's time to board.

As we will be sitting for quite some time, it's a good idea to get in as much exercise as possible before boarding. Walking can help get your circulation moving.

You might consider using this time as an opportunity to put yourself in a peaceful state with your essential oils (you have some with you in your carry-on bag) and music. Airports can be quite bustling with activity, but you can check into your own world with your oils and music. It's a good idea to check the Airport Departure signs often as you walk by them, just to make sure there are no surprises. It also can't hurt to walk by your gate several times to see what's going on, especially if you're on the standby list for an upgrade.

Airport Food

If all of that walking has made you hungry, and you're not headed to a wonderful meal in first class, then let's talk about some food options. Some airports are much better at providing healthy options than others. As a general theme, my default food is Asian, as they tend to use more vegetables and not a lot of wheat and dairy. There are downsides for sure but, in general, Asian food tends to be healthier than other options you'll find in an airport. One of the major issues with some Asian foods is that they tend to use a lot of sauce (most with sugar and MSG), so be sure to ask for "light on the sauce."

I used to go to Subway and order a 6" veggie sandwich on flatbread, as it had lots of veggies (I add the spinach and guacamole) and less bread. This is not a bad option except for the bread. Flat bread has a little less wheat than the other options. These days I'm trying to avoid all wheat if possible. You can also opt for the salad here or at other food places. Just make sure that you get the dressing on the side so that you can decide how much to use.

You can also find somewhat healthy snacks (i.e. with an ingredient list that you can recognize and a few grams of sugar) in some airports, as many have a place to get freshly squeezed juice, whole fruits, or nuts. I would avoid the frozen yogurt, as it is still dairy and has quite a bit of sugar in it. In general, try to look for places that sell "things that grow" – fruits, nuts, veggies, and very little grains. In general, grains are one or two metabolic steps away from sugar, and tend to cause issues with blood sugar regulation, so are treated a little differently than other "things that grow."

Summary

○ Opt out at airport security to avoid radiation

○ Register for Global Entry (if you travel internationally) and TSA PreCheck to avoid lines and extra radiation

○ Get some exercise by walking around the airport

○ Eat healthy airport food as required

Chapter 4

Thriving on the Airplane

Whew . . . you made it to your comfortable seat on the airplane. For discussion purposes, let's assume that you are in a coach seat, but if you made it to first or business class, then life might be a little more pleasant during your flight. The first thing you'll want to do is get out all of the things that you think you might need during the flight, and put the rest in the overhead bin nearest your seat. For long flights, you might put your shoes in the overhead bin to conserve space under the seat in front of you (if there's room up there, and if your feet don't create attention with their own unique smells). It's really nice to have as much room for your feet as possible, so get everything into the overhead bin if you can. This will allow you to move your feet around to keep the blood circulation in your body moving.

Hopefully you are in the best seat that you can possibly get. If not, then now is a good time to start looking around the plane. Every now and then, there will be a flight that is not completely full. As you get closer to the departure time, and especially after they close the airplane door, you might have the opportunity to change seats. If you see a preferable seat that is open, please ask your flight attendant if you can move to that seat. If it's at all possible, they will let you move. I remember being so thankful on a long flight to Chile, where I could get an open three-seat section so that I could lay down to sleep. It's not first class, but much better than scrunching up in a single chair.

I usually take out my plastic bag, tablet (e.g. iPad), and any magazines that I've brought with me and put them in the seat pocket in front of me. I typically put on my noise-canceling headphones as soon as I get in my seat and listen to peaceful music from my smartphone. You may also wish to listen to the audio (or video) from the airplane's entertainment system. For international flyers: make sure you have the correct adapter to plug into the audio system on the plane, as some planes require an adapter with two prongs. Sometimes I'll turn on the noise-canceling headphones without any music (just for the quiet), so

I can hear the announcements, especially if I'm in a foreign country. It can be quite entertaining. I like to use the small pillow as lumbar (lower back) support. Once you've built a comfortable nest, you can settle in for the flight.

It's nice to have a flashlight app available on your smartphone, so that if you drop anything during the flight (if it's dark), you'll have a way to find it. I was once on a long flight and my traveling neighbor dropped a pill that we would most likely not have found without this app.

> **From a health perspective, your main objective on the plane is to stay hydrated.**

From a health perspective, once you get on the plane, your main mission is to stay hydrated. All sorts of good things happen when your body gets enough water. Remember, that water is involved in almost all cellular activities in the body. Once the plane takes off, you are fighting against the dry air and high altitudes that naturally dehydrate the body. The longer the flight, the more important this becomes as dehydration plays a big part in many health issues. Unfortunately, this comes at a bit of a cost to you – namely, that you have to get lots of water, remember to drink it regularly, and then visit the lavatories more often than you might like. If you are fortunate enough to be seated in business or first class, you may want to be careful about the free food and drink. Remember, that alcohol actually dehydrates the body, so you'll want to drink extra water if you are drinking alcohol. You'll also have to be careful with the extra food temptations, like salty roasted peanuts.

Getting out of your seat to walk around is actually a good thing, as it helps to promote circulation. And DVT (deep vein thrombosis) is a real thing – it can be very painful and even life-threatening. You'll see the warnings in the airplane magazines and informational flyer in the seat back pocket about sitting too long, as it can be a real problem, especially on long flights. The DVT articles and pictures give you some great ideas on things you can do in your seat to minimize this issue, namely ankle/foot exercises. If DVT is something that you've been challenged with before, it might be a good idea to look into compression socks. There are also some essential oils that can help with circulation. You might try applying some YL Cypress and Eucalyptus oils to your feet and legs, either before the flight or in the lavatory during one of your visits. If you have issues with circulation in your legs, then you might want to consider using SP Collinsonia Root. If it were me, I'd take three capsules of SP Collinsonia Root followed by a full glass of water before the flight, another dose in the middle or end of the flight, and another dose right before bed that night. SP Collinsonia Root, also known as the stone root plant, is an old American Indian remedy for veins and circulation. It can be slightly hard on the stomach for some folks, which is why I recommend a large glass of water immediately after each dose.

From a germ perspective, the most "handled" items around you are the tray table, the arm rests, the remote (if you have one), and the magazines in front of you. I use my Thieves wipes and/or Thieves spray to clean off these areas, as this is now my "home away from home" for a few hours, and it would be best not to pick up any unwanted guests during my stay. I recently read some research that showed that some really nasty bugs (e.g. MRSA) remained on the tray tables (I've seen people changing their baby's diaper on them!), armrests, and other solid surfaces for several days, and they were still alive on the fabric seat pocket for up to a week. Be careful to look into the seat back pocket before reaching inside, as there may be things in there that you'd rather not touch. One other note: they also found that the airport kiosk where you get your plane tickets was fairly clean, but the security bins that you use to put your bags through the scanner were pretty contaminated.

The oils come in handy for other uses as well. I remember boarding a flight from Eastern Europe to London, and an older gentleman sat down in front of me. I didn't really notice until after he sat down, but a very strange odor surrounded our little area. Apparently, he hadn't bothered with a shower before the flight – or perhaps a few days prior. I pulled out my Peace & Calming oil blend and put a few drops on the back of his headrest and it created a wonderful shield for our little group. I saw several passengers nearby whisper "thank you" as we enjoyed the renewed air. You might also share some of your peaceful oils with the flight attendants – they can definitely use them at times.

I Can't Sleep on a Plane!

Now that you have your cozy nest all happy and clean, you may find yourself getting sleepy. You can only watch so many movies and read so many books before you start to feel drowsy. It is preferable to adapt to your destination's time zone as quickly as you can – preferably while you're on the plane. Even if you're on a domestic or red-eye (crossing the U.S. at night) flight and just want to take a quick nap, there are some things that can help.

I carry ear plugs and a sleep mask in my travel backpack. I put these in my pockets before boarding the plane, just to keep them handy. I know some travelers are big fans of prescription drugs that can help you sleep (e.g. Ambien), but as you might guess, I think it's better for the body to use natural support, if at all possible. I add a few (2 or 3) drops of PRL Melatonin to some water to help kick-start the sleep process. Melatonin is a hormone that is produced by the pineal gland, and it is secreted during your circadian wake/sleep cycle when it's time to go to bed (or your body thinks it's time for bed). Darkness is one of the things that will trigger this release. The pineal gland is situated in the middle of the brain and is affected by light/dark cycles. This is where the sleep mask comes in.

> **As a general sleep tip, I find it best to keep your bedroom as dark as possible. And if you have to get up in the middle of the night, do your best to keep your eyes closed and keep it dark (i.e. don't turn on the lights).**

Electricity has brought us all sorts of advantages, but unfortunately has completely destroyed our body's ability to stay in harmony with the light/dark, day/night cycles that are foundational to our health. So, taking a little melatonin, along with putting on your sleep mask, is a great way to kick-start the sleep process.

You might also consider using some of the essential oils you packed to help make you sleepy even faster. YL Lavender, YL Peace & Calming, or some of the other relaxing individual or oil blends can help the brain calm down and put you in a restful place. In terms of sounds, I find it best to either use earplugs to remove as much outside stimulation as possible, or noise canceling headphones so that you can listen to either peaceful music or some type of meditation sound track that can help you rest.

Even with this relaxing ritual, some of us (like me) have a hard time sleeping on an airplane. That's okay.

> **You don't actually have to fall asleep to allow your body to get the rest it needs.**

I call it "going into suspended animation." If you can do the things mentioned above, breathe and rest, your body will thank you for it . . . even if you only rest for 30 minutes.

Food on the Plane

If you are on a domestic flight, you may have been able to bring enough food with you so that you are not at the mercy of the airlines for a meal. If you are in first class, the food is pretty good, but you still have to be careful. They usually don't offer many choices. Also, in a previous chapter, we talked about the possibility of updating your travel profile with a special meal.

As a general health tip, it's not a good idea to drink liquids with your meal, as they dilute the digestive enzymes that your body is making to help digest your food. You can drink more than 15 minutes prior, or an hour or so later, but try to minimize drinking any liquids with your meal as you can. It's also ideal to drink liquids that are closer to room temperature (or warm/hot), as your body can assimilate these more easily (this advice comes primarily from Oriental medicine). You may want to use a few drops (1-3) of YL DiGize in a little water (or placed in a capsule) after your meal to help remove pathogens in the food you just ate. This is not a license to eat junk food and think that these drops will magically make the food more nutritious, but rather to help with any unwanted guests, as well as to assist your digestive system in assimilating the food.

Summary

○ Get on the plane as soon as you can

○ Use your noise-canceling headphones as much as possible

○ Drink as much water as you can throughout the flight

○ Sanitize around your seat area as much as possible – tray table, armrests, remote, etc.

○ Do ankle/foot exercises throughout the flight

○ Get up and walk around, if only to the lavatory

○ Find a rest/sleep routine that works for you – your body will reward you later

○ Use enzymes and oils to help digest your meal

Chapter 5

Adventures in Time Zones

While it can be very exciting to travel to destinations half way around the world, the impact of changes in time zones can be quite challenging for the body. For some people, just a one-hour shift in time (e.g. daylight savings time changes twice a year in the U.S.) can throw the body's clock off for a week. So, this chapter is not only for the twelve-hour time zone change, but also for those traveling to cities where there is only a few hours difference.

The effects of jet lag can really alter your plans to conquer the city upon arrival. If you don't know what I'm talking about, then you have probably not experienced serious jet lag. The most common symptoms include fatigue, confusion, and lack of awareness . . . not to mention drowsiness. For some people, these symptoms can last for several days or longer, so anything you do to lessen these effects is going to be a good thing for you. There have been recent studies that show that jet lag has also been shown to impact other areas of health, like decreasing memory capacity and the immune system, altering genes, inducing stress, and disturbing other brain functions.

Our bodies function best when we are in rhythm with the cycles of the planet. It is best if we can go to sleep when the sun goes down and wake up in the morning for the sunrise. The invention and subsequent pervasiveness of electric lights (and other electronic entertainment) has given us the freedom to alter these cycles dramatically. We can now stay up until after midnight with all of the lights on in the house and sleep later in the morning, but this is not ideal for our body. Sleep issues are prevalent in our society, and I believe that this is one of the main causes (among other things – stress being at the top). If we can live in harmony with the planet, as the human body has been accustomed to for many generations, then we are much more likely to live in a healthy state. Working nightshifts and sleeping during the day might be good for vampires, but not so much for you and me. All this to say, if you can remain in sync with the time zone that you are in, you will be less stressed, more productive, and much happier. Our mission, then, is to figure out how to get in sync with our destination time zone as quickly and comfortably as we possibly can.

If you are not traveling through more than three time zones, stay on your home time zone during your trip. For example, if you are flying from Texas to California (two-hour time difference), just keep your watch, body clock, and routine set to Texas time, if you can. This will obviously depend on the schedule at your destination and the length of time that you'll be there.

Adjusting Your Body Clock

Most people have a much more difficult time traveling from west to east. For me, flying from Texas to Europe is quite a challenge, as the flights typically leave late in the afternoon and arrive early the next morning. This might not be as bad if you can sleep on a plane, but for those of us who are merely resting, it's a bit more challenging. Some people have reported success with changing their body clock gradually before leaving for their trip, starting a few days prior to departure. I have not personally tried this but wanted to mention it as an option if you'd like to give it a try. You would basically go to bed earlier or later, depending on your direction of travel, and adjust a few hours per day, starting a week or so before your trip.

Flying East

I use several natural health strategies to help me adjust, once I get on the airplane. Let's say for example that I am traveling from Chicago to London (one of the more difficult directions and time zone changes) and that my flight departs around 6:00 PM (18:00 for my non-U.S. friends) and arrives in London around 8:00 AM the next morning. During half of the year, it is a six-hour time zone difference. The first thing I do when I get on the plane (literally when I step on it) is tell my mind that it is now six hours later. So, if we board at 5:30 PM, I will completely change my mindset to believing that it's 11:30 PM. Part of the challenge with this is that most international flights like to show the time of your departure and arrival city on the airplane monitors. I do not look at those and just completely imagine that I am in the destination city's time zone. I don't wear a watch, so I set my cell phone to London time and use that to keep track of my journey while I'm in the air. Another challenge is that when they serve dinner, you're really eating around 1:30 AM, but stay with me here.

As soon as I get to my seat and get everything settled, I put the packet of **No Jet Lag** (homeopathic remedy) in my pocket or the seat back pocket so that it's handy. Per the directions, you'll want to chew one of the tablets at take-off. Remember, as with all homeopathics, you will want to avoid eating or drinking within at least 20 minutes on either side of taking them.

Homeopathy is one of the original energy medicines, and while not traditionally accepted in the U.S., it is used quite extensively in other parts of the world and can be quite effective. Homeopathy operates on a "like cures like" principle that has been used for more than 200 years and is now confirmed by an increasing number of research publications. This means that a patient suffering from symptoms can be treated by micro-doses of a substance capable of producing similar symptoms in a healthy person. Homeopathic medicines stimulate the body's physiological reactions that restore health, with a very low risk of side effects due to the use of micro-doses.

The **No Jet Lag** directions say that you should chew one tablet at the time of each take-off, another every two hours in flight, and another after each landing (including at intermediate stops). During long flights, the two-hour intervals may be extended if the user is sleeping. I follow these directions and have found this remedy to be very effective.

EFT Tapping

So, we have set our "mind clock" to London time and taken our **No Jet Lag.** The next step that I do is practice an amazing energy system called EFT (Emotional Freedom Technique).

EFT[4] was developed by Gary Craig and is an extremely effective technique to help the body remove energy blockages and adapt. It can be used for a wide variety of health issues like pain (chronic and acute), depression, anxiety, motion sickness, and many, many others. I would encourage you to explore this amazing technique and how it can help you. It is basically a system of tapping certain acupuncture points around the face, neck, and hands, while saying certain phrases.

I usually take my first trip to the lavatory to do the tapping. You can do it in your seat, but people might give you some interesting looks, and I don't like to put a spotlight on myself before we've even taken off. I'll wait until I get my oils out and waft some smells around, and then when they start staring I'll start tapping.

There are basically nine key points that we will tap on the body. Start by putting all of the tips of the fingers of your right hand (could also use your left fingers) together to form one big "super tip". We will begin by tapping on the top of the head, near the center.

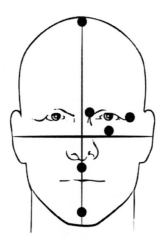

If it's now 7:00 PM, tap on that point, and say to yourself something like: "My body clock is now set to 1:00 AM. It's one o'clock in the morning." Then move to the face points and tap on each of them while repeating the statement(s) above. After you have completed all five of the face points, tap on the collarbone point, followed by the point underneath the arm.

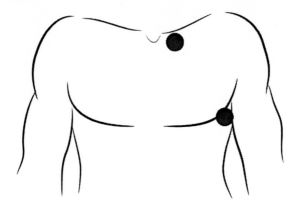

You can complete the sequence by tapping on the hand point.

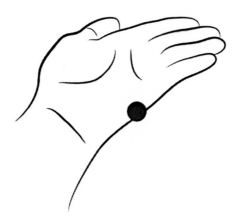

Here is a link to a video where I demonstrate the EFT tapping technique: http://tinyurl.com/o6chgye.

After you have completed tapping all nine points, you will take a deep breath to integrate the changes, and you are done with this round. I will continue to do this every time I visit the lavatory, and sometimes in my seat. You can't do it too often (other than the consequences of stares from your neighbors).

One of the healing arts that I study is a discipline called **Jin Shin Jyutsu[5].** It is an absolutely fascinating and amazing system that came from Japan and can help to balance disharmony in the body using a variety of hands-on techniques.

One of the most appealing aspects of Jin Shin Jyutsu is the ability to use "self-help" techniques to balance your own body.

There are several techniques from Jin Shin Jyutsu that can help our bodies to more easily adapt to these changes in time zones. Jin Shin Jyutsu self-help techniques can be likened to closing an energy circuit in the body, helping it to harmonize.

One of the best things that you can do to help your body regain harmony (even beyond jet lag) is to simply hold your fingers.

Start by holding your left little finger (for example) with your right hand. Wrap the finger as much as possible with the right hand with the right index finger side nearest the knuckles of the left little finger. Hold this finger for several minutes (really up to you), and then move to holding the ring finger. Continue to hold all ten fingers in succession and breathe deeply until you've held all ten fingers. You can repeat this as often as you like throughout the flight and beyond, as it can help with more than just jet lag.

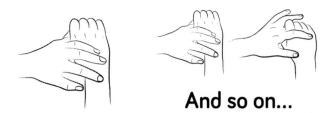

And so on...

Here is a link to a video where I demonstrate the Jin Shin Jyutsu hand positions:

http://tinyurl.com/p35axrk.

Another technique to help the body adapt to time changes is to sit on your hands. You can either sit on the palms or the back of the hands, preferably near the "sit bones" (you'll feel them if you don't know what I'm talking about). You can remain in this position for as long as you feel comfortable, and can repeat as often as you like.

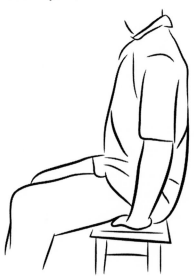

I usually start watching a movie after take-off, and just pretend that I'm enjoying a late night party with friends (since it's "really" so early in the morning) as the flight attendants bring dinner. Once they have finished the service, the movie is over, and I've visited the lavatory, I'll begin my bedtime flight routine.

Bedtime Flight Routine

The first thing I do is take out my bottle of PRL Melatonin and put two or three drops in a small amount of water. I like the PRL Melatonin, as it is in a pure source liquid form, so will act quickly in the body. Sometimes I put a little water in the small lid on my bottled water and add the drops (if I don't have a cup handy). Or, if you prefer, you can also swallow one or two YL Sleep Essence gel caps (instead of the PRL Melatonin) that are a combination of relaxing essential oils and melatonin. Next, I like to get out my YL Peace & Calming (or your favorite relaxing oils or blends), and put a few drops in my palms. I rub my palms together, cup them over my nose, and take a deep breath. We are now setting the stage for sleep, or at least, rest. I then pull out my sleep mask, cover myself with the blanket (seatbelt on the outside) and either use the ear plugs or the noise canceling headphones. You can listen to relaxing music or guided meditations, or whatever makes you feel comfortable and happy. Even if I can't sleep, I'll do my best to lie there quietly for several hours at least. If you are simply resting, don't forget to take your **No Jet Lag** pills and drink some water every now and then.

As we approach London, people start opening their windows, and the sunlight bursts through. I'd like to tell you that when that happens I usually feel refreshed and ready to start my new day. But at least for me, that is usually not the case. It might be for those who can sleep on a plane. So I remind myself that light exposure is one of my best friends, as it helps my body sync with the earth's rhythm and to my new home away from home.

Once you arrive on the ground at your destination, continue taking the **No Jet Lag** homeopathics for a few more hours after landing. It just helps your body to avoid some of the symptoms of jet lag. You'll also want to continue doing the EFT tapping as often as you can upon arrival (it only takes a few minutes).

When you get to your hotel, check around for some grass. What? Along with light, one of the best ways to sync your body with the earth is to stand on it, preferably with bare feet. I know that this can be somewhat of a challenge depending on where you are.

> **We now know from much research that standing barefoot on the earth (called Earthing) is known to help balance the energy channels of the body and sync with the natural biorhythms of the earth's energy.**

It will also help your body sync to your local time zone much easier. It would be ideal if you could stand on the earth for at least 15 minutes . . . longer is better.

If you have chronic pain or other health issues, you might consider standing or sitting with your bare feet on some earth – preferably wet grass (as it is a better conductor). Modern society and the invention of rubber-soled shoes has put yet another large wedge between us and the planet that supports us. It is in our best interest to connect to the ground as often as we can. The more you can do this at your destination, the better in terms of easing your jet lag. Walking on the beach is also fantastic, but those sites rarely come up on business trips.

You can also purchase a grounding mat or grounding sheets to use on your trip (and at home). These plug into the third prong on most U.S. electrical outlets (and are available on many international outlets as well) which connect to a grounding rod outside of the building. You can just place the mat on the ground and put your bare feet on it to get similar effects. This is good if you are in a city that doesn't have a lot of grass, or you don't have time to walk around. You can also use the grounding sheets on the bed to sync you up while you sleep.

Noon is a special time and links with the heart meridian (energy channel of the heart from Chinese acupuncture). Meridians are the fiber optic light channels of energy that run throughout our body. The twelve different organ systems of the body are associated with different times of day, and the heart channel "starts working" typically around noon. If you have the chance, go outside, stand on the earth, look toward the sun, and trace your fingers up your arm starting at the tip of your little finger on the outside of the arm all the way up and to your heart. This is the approximate path of this meridian. This is yet another way to help your body to sync to this time zone.

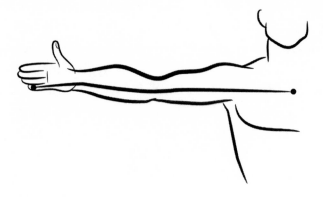

Here is a link to a video where I discuss tracing the heart meridian: http://tinyurl.com/mcyprcn.

Don't forget to continue drinking lots of filtered water, as this will also help your body adjust. Depending on how you are feeling, you might consider taking one or two tablets of SP St John's Wort, as it can also help with the symptoms. I try not to take this unless needed, but it can be very helpful if you find yourself suffering from the nasty symptoms of jet lag.

Depending on where you are (and where you flew in from), your next task is to stay awake until 9:00 PM (21:00) that night. If I am on a long flight that arrives early in the morning, I will book the hotel room for the night before, so that I can check in and take a nap. Be careful to limit this nap to no more than 90 minutes. I know that you can get very sleepy in the afternoon, but do whatever it takes to stay up until at least 9:00 PM (target 10:00 PM, if that helps), especially on that first night, and you'll be glad you did. One very helpful idea is to keep moving. Go take a walk around the city (assuming it's safe to do so) or around a mall to help you stay awake. I usually don't drink coffee, but might have a cup (or some black tea) as a last resort around 3:00 or 4:00 PM, at the latest (don't want it to keep me awake when I do go to bed).

You can also use invigorating essential oils like peppermint and eucalyptus to help you stay awake. You can dilute as necessary and apply to the temples, thymus area (just above the center of your chest), and bottoms of the feet. I like to put a few drops of peppermint on my palms, rub them together, cup them over my nose, and breathe. Be careful not to get any in your eyes, or you'll be *really* awake, and not in a good way.

It is typically easier to stay awake until 9:00 PM if you are out with friends. Once you get back to your room and it's quiet, it can be quite difficult to keep your eyes open. But, once it's time for bed, follow the bedtime routine mentioned earlier using the melatonin and calming oils. I do not recommend using supplemental melatonin every night, but it's definitely okay as you adjust to and from the time zones of your trip, as needed.

Some trips are easier than others to acclimate. I can usually sync up to the local time zone pretty quickly (one day) if I follow the steps above, but others can take much longer. I know that trips from Asia to the U.S. require much longer for me, as it can take a week or so to get truly back in sync. Your flight often arrives home before the time that you left. So if you depart from China at 4:30 PM on a Wednesday, you may arrive home at 4:00 PM that same day . . . very strange. I remember one trip where I was flying from Beijing and was scheduled to land around 3:00 PM on a Saturday. My daughter had a ballet recital that night (gotta love the timing), so I challenged myself to stay awake in a dark auditorium. I'm just happy that I made it, but it was not the most ideal situation.

You will want to follow all of these steps for your return trip as well, including staying awake until 9:00 PM.

Summary

○ If your trip takes you through less than three time zones, stay in your local time

○ Change your mind set to focus on the destination time zone as soon as you get on the plane

○ Take your homeopathic remedies to help your body clear symptoms

○ Get outside in the sun as much as possible

○ Stand with bare feet on the earth as much as possible (wet grass and beach are best)

○ Use your Jin Shin Jyutsu and EFT techniques

○ Stay awake until at least 9:00 PM in your new destination (and when returning home)

Chapter 6

Your Home Away from Home:

The Hotel Room

Hotel Arrival

You finally pull up to your beautiful hotel (sometimes to realize that it doesn't really look like the pictures on their website) and are all ready to get to your room. As you approach the hotel check-in area, you'll want to be aware of a few things. As you sign in, be aware that *many* other hotel guests (from all over the world) have probably used that same pen at the front desk, so please use your own pen, or make sure to use the Thieves hand sanitizer after signing, so you don't begin your hotel stay with unwanted guests.

The Room

Once I get to my room, the first thing I like to do is get out my smartphone and take a picture of the room number. This way I won't have to rack my brain to remember. I also check the bed for bed bugs. Now I know that many of you don't want to do this, but you certainly don't want these critters sharing the room with you, or worse, joining you for your trip home. They are small, brown, wingless insects around the size of apple seeds, but if you lift up the top mattress a little you should be able to see them (or possibly black specks that could indicate their droppings) on white sheets. If you do see them, call the front desk and ask for another room immediately. Like ticks and mosquitoes, bed bugs feed on mammalian blood. They are smart and know how to hide in bedding, wait until nightfall and feed on sleeping humans and animals. If you don't see any bugs, it's still a good idea to spray some Thieves oil and Purification oil on the bed, just for precaution. These two blends will help to remove them. You can mix five or so drops of each of these two oils in a spray bottle with some water and spray the sheets.

Energy/EMFs

I like to move the alarm clock as far away from the bed as possible. Anything with an electrical connection has the ability to impact our body, especially as you are lying there eight plus hours a night. The EMFs (electromagnetic frequencies) can definitely impact the body in a variety of ways, most of which are not beneficial.

Speaking of EMFs and the energetics of your room, there are some things that you can do to make the room "feel better." Now, I know this may seem a little strange (just so you think I don't know), but the energetics of the room can have a huge impact on how you feel – anxious, nervous, edgy, wound up, etc. It can also play a part in helping your immune system (and you) to stay as healthy as possible. Here are some easy energy housekeeping ideas that I recommend:

• Unplug the telephone by the bed – this just removes one more electrical item from around your sleeping area.

• If the mirror is opposite your bed (i.e. you can see yourself in the mirror when lying down), then cover it with a towel. Basic Feng Shui and Vastu concepts tell us that mirrors reflect energy, and you don't want that happening while you're trying to sleep.

• Unplug the television (if you're not planning to watch it).

• Move the bedside lamp as far away from your head as possible.

- Sleep on the side of the bed that is farthest away from the clock radio and lamp.

- Use an alarm on your cell phone for waking up, but keep the cell phone on the table across the room.

I use a PRL Pyrafire pyramid[6] to help remediate the energetics in the room. You can purchase a small one on my website, or search on the Internet. This will basically create a positive energetic atmosphere and remediate the space (i.e. make it more compatible with your body), as well as EMFs like WiFi and wiring in the wall. I place the pyramid about three feet off the ground and a foot from a wall on a natural surface (wood or glass is best). If I use the maid service, I will put my pyramid in the safe every day before I leave, or even better, just take it with me in my backpack so that I can use it at the office (or wherever I am going).

Settle in

I like to use the hotel safe (if they have one), as it's a good idea to keep your valuables in here throughout your stay. I keep my headphones, pyramid, passport, one shoe, and other valuables here when I'm not in the room. One word of caution, and this is why the shoe is in there - don't forget to empty the safe when you check out! I learned this lesson on one of my favorite trips to New Zealand. I have to say that this is one of the most amazing places on the planet, but I'm trying not to be too biased. I had packed my things and was in the cab back to the airport in Auckland (a 45 minute drive from the hotel), thinking about the wonderful time I'd had there and all of the amazing Kiwi friends that I'd made. I had given myself plenty of time to make my flight just in case there was traffic and just enjoyed the ride.

As soon as the driver pulled into the airport I had a sinking feeling in my stomach. I frantically searched through my backpack but visualized my passport, completely secure back in the hotel safe in my room! You have to know that if you're going to pull a crazy, stressful stunt like this, New Zealand (and for that matter, Australia) would be the place to do it. The Kiwis and Aussies are so laid back in their personalities that just being around them calms you down. I told the driver what had happened, and of course he said, "No worries." He loaned me his cell phone and I called the hotel. They sent someone up to my room and called us right back, as they did indeed find my passport in the safe.

Since we did not have enough time to go back to the hotel and return to make my flight, the driver called a friend of his that went to the hotel, picked up my passport and brought it to me at the airport. The next 45 minutes or so, I just sat there praying and hoping that a "driver" would show up with my passport, as otherwise, I would be in New Zealand for another day. Sure enough, he did, and you can probably feel the sigh of relief with me as you read this. I made my flight and indeed it was "no worries," as I spent that 45 minutes focused on how to release worry and have faith. That experience taught me a valuable lesson. I always put a shoe in my hotel safe, as it's a little more obvious when you don't have a pair of shoes when packing to go home.

From a hygiene perspective, it's always a good idea to use your Thieves spray and/or wipes to clean off the TV remote (if you're going to watch TV), light switches, door knobs, pens in the room and, of course, the bathroom. The cleaners that the maids use in the bathrooms are usually not the most toxin-free, so it's better if you can wipe things down yourself, and just ask for new towels as needed (rather than maid service every day). If you choose not to get the maid service, just hang the Do Not Disturb sign on the door.

I know that the free soap, shampoo, and conditioners are sometimes alluring, but keep in mind that they are not normally purchased for their health qualities (though sometimes they are better at higher end hotels). It's better to use the toiletries that you brought from home.

If you packed an essential oil diffuser, this would be a good time to break that out and get some good smells (and disinfectants) going in the room. If not, you can put a few drops of an essential oil or two on a cotton ball and place it in the vent so that the air will be forced through it. Another option is to bring an empty spray bottle and fill it with water and a few drops of oil (maybe 5-10 per spray bottle) to make your own room freshener. Then you can spray around as needed. Good oils to use for this are YL Purification, YL Thieves, or YL Lemon.

Water

One thing that you'll definitely want to explore at this point is the search for water. We all know that some destinations have questionable water quality, and I don't advise drinking out of the faucet either way. But, you'll want to know those places where you need to use bottled water to brush your teeth. You can ask them at the front desk, and they'll tell you if the water in the hotel is filtered, in which case it's probably okay to use it to brush your teeth.

If the hotel gives you a free bottle of water (or two), it's probably a good sign that the water in that city is not the safest to drink.

If you do get free water bottles, they will usually restock them for you for free (with maid service, or if you ask at the front desk). If you go the maid service route, make sure you move the bottles each day into a drawer or in the closet so that they'll continue restocking and you'll be taken care of for water during your stay.

One of the first things I do once I get settled is figure out where I can get and continue getting good drinking water. If the hotel provides the bottled water as I just mentioned, you may be all set. You should still have your plastic water bottle from the plane, so you can fill it back up with good quality water. It's also a good idea to drink from your bottle as we're not quite sure just how sanitary the drinking glasses actually are in a hotel room (though many of us have seen videos and news reports that might make you think twice about drinking out of the glasses in a hotel room).

One of my favorite tips is to visit the health club in the hotel as soon as possible, as they usually have a filtered drinking water dispenser in that room. It might feel a little awkward walking in and just taking water, but if the health club is part of your room charge, it's okay to use it – even if only for water.

Another option is to ask the front desk if there is a convenience store near the hotel. I remember checking into a hotel in Istanbul and walking for 10 minutes across a very busy street and up and down hills to get to a place where I could buy water. I bought a six-pack of large water bottles (enough to last me a week) and trekked back to the hotel. You can get very thirsty that first night (after flying), so it's good to have this water on hand in case you wake up in the middle of the night with a dry mouth.

Now that you have a good supply of water, find a way to heat it up. Most hotels around the world have an electric kettle (or coffee maker) in the room. If not, call the front desk and ask for one. If you have a way to boil your water, you can now use the oatmeal, soups, and other goodies that you brought from home, as needed.

After getting all of the above items checked off the list, I like to do a little personal hygiene. I take a nice hot shower and use a neti pot to rinse out my sinuses from the long flight. You can search on the Internet for videos that show you how to use the neti pot. You will want to heat up some of your drinking water for this, and add a teaspoon or so of sea salt to clean your sinuses.

If you have the time, one of the best things you can do after a long flight is to get a foot massage. Depending on where you are, there might be a local place nearby (especially if you are in Asia – they are the best) that you can walk to as hotels are not known for low-cost spa treatments. If you don't want to get a foot massage, you can use the golf or tennis balls that you brought with you. Just place them on the floor and roll them around with the bottoms of your feet – your own personal foot massagers.

Once it's time for bed, it's a good idea to have some peaceful music playing and get out your calming oils. If you'd like a fair chance at a good night's sleep, this is not the time to watch that suspense thriller on TV, as light reading might be a better idea. I like to use YL Peace & Calming or Lavender (or another calming oil or blend) on the bottom of my feet to help me sleep. Add a few drops to your palms and rub across the bottoms of the feet.

It's best to sleep with the room as dark as possible (to aid your body's production of melatonin), so close the curtains all the way to keep as much light out as possible. The curtains in some hotel rooms don't close all the way, so bring a large binder clip (the front desk might have one if you didn't bring one) that you can use to close the gap and help block out the outside light. I may also get one of the towels from the bathroom and place it under the front door to block out light from the hall if it's really bright and there is a big gap under the door. I also use a sleep mask if I can't get the room dark enough. Studies have shown that we typically sleep better in a cooler room, so once you are ready for bed, turn that thermostat down to a nice, cool temperature.

You might also consider taking a few drops of PRL Melatonin or YL Sleep Essence (blend of essential oils with a little melatonin added – I use one or two gel caps), especially on the first night as you get acclimated. If you usually get up to go to the bathroom at night, see if you can find a small light (or pack a night light) to help you find your way, as turning on the bright bathroom lights will shut down your melatonin production, and it might be more difficult to go back to sleep.

As you go to sleep, you might have the joy of being entertained by exciting noises like traffic from the streets below, neighbors, nearby alarm clocks, rowdy partiers, dripping faucets, and other fun-filled sounds. As with the plane, you might consider using your ear plugs or noise-canceling headphones with some meditation music. You might also get a white noise app for your smartphone – either played through the headphones or just playing through its speaker – that will make just enough noise to cancel out the local sounds. One last thing before you drift off . . . don't forget to add a few prayers of gratitude for the safe journey that ended in your hotel bed. It didn't have to be that way.

Mini-bar

No chapter on the hotel room would be complete without at least mentioning the mini-bar. For many, the mini-bar can be quite the delight, especially when you're hungry after a long flight. I do not personally look at the items in the mini-bar, as I know how unhealthy and overpriced they can be. I have been charged for things before, even though I didn't consume them. This is when I learned that the newer hotels have weight sensitive measuring systems – so when you move the item (even if you put it back), it automatically sends the charge through to your bill. From a health perspective, I think we can do better in packing our own "just in case" foods and avoid these snacks on a tray.

> **As you spend time throughout your trip, don't forget to update your packing list with any items that you wish you had, or that you had to buy. This updated packing list can be your best friend when traveling!**

When it's time to pack up and go home, put your dirty clothes in plastic bags, just in case you managed to pick up some unwanted guests (bed bugs). Sort through all of your checked baggage items into your bag, and get your "on the plane" items ready to go as you did when you started the trip. I like to roll all of my dirty clothes into "burrito rolls" as it tends to take up less room. And, if you're like me, you'll need to have more room for the souvenirs for the kids. When our twins were younger, they would offer to help me unpack as soon as I got home, looking for hidden treasures in my luggage.

Social Media

With the rise of social media comes the need to update all of your friends on everything that you're doing – especially if it's something interesting like traveling. The challenge with this is that you can become so consumed with taking and posting interesting pictures for your Facebook page that you miss out on some of the time that you could be using to explore your destination. There is no problem with taking pictures, but you might want to wait until you get back from your trip to do the editing and posting. Whenever I traveled to ANY city, I assumed that I would never have the opportunity to return there again, so I wanted to use as much time as possible to explore and see at least all of the highlights.

One other thing to consider is that if you are posting pictures on the Internet from a distant location, you are potentially telling "the world" that you are not at home, which could lead to safety issues (e.g. burglary). There is so much we don't know about who is looking at the information that we post on the Internet, so be careful.

Here is an interesting story that captures this point:

The Gift

by Leo Babauta

Three people are given a magical gift by a luminous, kindhearted fairy. The gift is that for just one hour, they get to experience magic and wonders. This limited time is filled with visual delights, food of the utmost deliciousness, amazing people with incredible talents, and love.

The first person is a great man, and while he's grateful for the gift, he has lots to do and so regrettably has to spend a lot of it replying to emails and texts, and checking for updates in social media. He does take some pictures of the delicious food and shares it on social media, though he doesn't pay attention to the taste.

The second person is a bit of procrastinator (okay, let's be honest: a big procrastinator), and while she really wants to use this gift wisely,

---

she keeps putting it off. She spends much of the hour watching videos the first guy posts online of the magical world, but she doesn't go out and experience it herself.

The third person is blown away by this gift. What an incredible opportunity! She realizes she needs to make the most of it, but isn't sure how. So she starts by paying attention. She notices every little detail. She listens to the amazing people she meets, and tries to really see them for who they are. She tastes the food and pays close attention to every sensation as she eats, savoring the food slowly. She then practices gratitude for every moment, every person, everything she's given. She's filled with happiness by every little thing in this hour. Finally, she changes people's lives. She uses what's left of this dwindling hour to learn magic skills, to heal people who are struggling (including the first guy), to make things to delight the other amazing people in this magical world. She becomes the gift for others.

The hour is over, and the first two people realize they've wasted the gift, and will never get it again. They're filled with regret. The third person has no regrets, because she paid attention, was grateful, and used the magic to change lives. She used the gift to its fullest potential.

Which of those three people are you?

Summary

○ Be aware of and disinfect items that have been handled by others – pens, remotes, etc.

○ Check your room for things that would require you to move before you unpack, like bed bugs

○ Find a good source of drinking water for your stay

○ Get your room set up to support you energetically – move things around, diffuse oils, position your pyramid, etc.

○ Find a good bedtime routine that works for you – oils, bath, music, dark, sounds, etc.

○ Update your packing list as you go

○ Prepare a social media plan that will allow you to focus on your trip

Chapter 7

What Can I Eat While Traveling?

Here's the chapter that most people think about when they hear about a book on tips for traveling healthy. If you are a healthy eater at home, then your challenges with eating healthy while traveling are probably more of an awareness issue than anything else. If you are not a healthy eater at home, then it's doubtful that a trip will change everything for you, but you never know. As with most things in this book, I will describe a spectrum of possibilities from domestic travel (where you have less issues with foods foreign to you), to international travel (where each meal can be an adventure). The other spectrum, of course, is from the fried chicken and ice cream traveler to the raw-food-vegan. I will do my best to provide a few tips for each type of traveler.

We know that the immune system predominantly resides in the digestive tract, so it stands to reason that eating healthy foods will go a long way in helping us get and keep a healthy immune system. This is a universal statement, not just for when you are traveling. Your immune system is the foundation for health, as it keeps things in balance in your body (keeps the good guys in and the bad guys out – and everyone in balance).

There has been much research recently on the balanced microbiome in the gut. I like to think of this as the rainforest in your tummy. It's the balance of the diversity that is the key. Research has shown that bacteria outnumber our "human" cells by a factor of at least ten to one. You may have to ponder on that a bit to realize that the balance of bacteria (and other critters) in our body is much different than previously thought.

> **Many people believe that we want to get rid of all the bacteria, viruses, and fungi in our body, but the reality is that they all serve a purpose – when they are in balance.**

The key to this is to maintain an ecosystem that supports the proper balance of good guys and bad guys. For example, when you take a prescription antibiotic, it can remove most of the "bad" bacteria that the doctor is shooting for, but it also removes the good guys as well, which is why you should always take a good probiotic (meaning "for life") with any antibiotic (meaning "against life") to attempt to keep things in balance. There is a time and a place for prescription pharmaceuticals, but I would only use them as a last resort. In some cases, prescription drugs can definitely save lives, but you have to do your homework, as there can be many side effects. The point of all of this is that the majority of your ability to stay happy and healthy when traveling resides in your immune system . . . which is foundationally dependent on the health and balance of your digestive system. As mentioned earlier in the book, we know that stress (sometimes increased when traveling) can impact our immune system in a negative way, so we need to do some extra things to help keep it functioning effectively.

Our fundamental need for daily survival is energy.

We really need the energy of the sun, and if we could just eat solar energy, that would be great. There are people who get their energy from the sun only by staring at it . . . really! They are called "breatharians" and you might want to look them up on the Internet, if you're interested. This practice is obviously not for everyone, but just shows that the body can function with very little food when required. We can only live for a few minutes without air, a few days without water, but several weeks without food. Back to the sun. It supports all life on our planet, including us. Since we can't eat the sun, we use our friends, the plants, to help us. As you might remember from elementary school, plants capture the energy of the sun, using photosynthesis, and store it in their plant bodies. When we eat these non-toxic fruits and vegetables, we are getting this energy along with the myriad phytonutrients (plant nutrients) stored in each specific plant. This is the foundation of natural healing – using energy from plants, herbs, and other natural substances to aid the body in its healing.

So what does all of this have to do with eating on my trip? Well, all of the above is background to say that your body will be the most happy and healthy if you will eat a diet that is primarily based on fruits and vegetables.

> **Quite simply –**
>
> **eat things that grow.**

We need to eat somewhere between 10-14 servings per day of nutritious, organic produce in order to stay healthy. This can be quite challenging, especially while traveling, which is why I'm a big fan of Juice Plus+. These supplements are basically fruits, vegetables, grapes, and berries in a capsule or chewable. Check out the link[7] at the back of the book for more information.

If you'd rather have something other than JP, I'd recommend a good quality, whole food supplement, as opposed to a synthetic, isolated "vitamin," such as (1,000 mg of Vitamin C or 50 mg of Vitamin B6). In my opinion, whole foods are more beneficial to the body than isolated vitamins, as whole foods are in their natural whole form – with all of their cofactors in place. Our bodies have evolved to digest and utilize food, not so much with isolated vitamins. There is place for high dose specific nutrients (e.g. 20,000 mg of Vitamin C), but as a general practice, I like whole food supplements, such as JP. I also do my best to limit the amount of supplements I have to take with me when traveling, and whole food versions tend to help with this.

Besides taking Juice Plus+ daily (think of it as an insurance policy to bridge the gap), I do my best to eat as many fruits and vegetables as I can. I personally limit my meat intake to a few times per week, and then mostly eat turkey, chicken, or fish. Fish is an amazingly nutritious food, but unfortunately we have contaminated the oceans so much that much of our seafood is loaded with toxins, like heavy metals. This doesn't include the farm raised fish in tanks (usually tilapia), which can be even worse due to the GMO foods that they are typically fed.

There are many books[9] written on which diet you should choose and why, but I'm just going to suggest that you work on eating as many fruits and veggies as you can, and limit a few things that are known to hinder the immune system.

The three main items that I'll ask you to consider limiting while on your trip are sugar, dairy, and wheat.

For those of you who like a soda or beer with your cheese pizza, this might be quite challenging. If you can severely limit or avoid these foods, you'll be much better off in the long run (and even in the short run).

Now, I do have to include a balanced perspective here and say that I think it's important to indulge in the local delicacy at your destination. You don't want to travel halfway around the world and not try the *trdnelnik,* for example, in the Czech Republic. Or the dim sum in China. But, try to limit your local cuisine indulgences to a reasonable amount, if it's in the "not so good for you" category.

It's all about balance.

One of the main things that I've learned in my Aikido practice is the importance of balance. It is very difficult to respond to others who are attacking you, if you are physically and/or mentally off balance. Aikido teaches us to use movement and techniques to keep ourselves in balance relative to our opponents, both on and off the mat. I have used the principles of Aikido in my everyday work world as well, as I might have to deal with less than pleasant personalities. We learn to deflect and move and allow balance to settle between us. If you have never seen Aikido in action, you might be interested in watching a few videos on the Internet.

When it comes to the spectrum, I am more of a balanced traveler – you may catch me eating some "hey that's not good for you" things like desserts (who can pass up a French éclair or New York cheesecake?), but I balance desserts with extra veggies and lots of clean water throughout the trip. It's kind of like doing extra exercise before and after your trip. I enjoy my travels to the degree that I can, but keep it in balance. I know that this approach to eating might surprise some health purists, and I'm not saying that I eat whatever I want . . . but rather that I don't want to miss out on local cuisine because it doesn't fit a restricted diet.

When I went to Mexico City for the first time I was on "high caution" due to the stories of not-so-pleasant, digestive disasters. But after being there for a week with my new friends, they took me to a restaurant and suggested that I try the *escamoles.* Hmmm . . . I asked what that was, and of course they said, "Just try it." Double hmmm. As a sometimes adventurous guy, I did and they were actually pretty good. So what are *escamoles?* Giant ant eggs (and you can only get them during the rainy season). Ah, the things we'll try when we are visitors.

Food Toxins

One of the biggest challenges that you'll have when traveling in some countries is the quality of the food that you'll eat. Even if you're doing a good job of eating fruits and vegetables, you still might run into some issues if the water is predominantly not healthy at your destination. I'm talking about the cities where you really need to use bottled water to brush your teeth. If this is the case, you have to remain diligent whenever you put anything in your mouth, thinking about if it came into contact with that water. For example, you might think that eating a salad with raw veggies would be good, and it usually is, but if it was washed with contaminated water, then you might as well drink a glass of bad water from the tap, you risk having stomach issues just the same. Most hotels and some restaurants in these types of locations use filtered water . . . but be careful and ask a lot of questions.

Boiling water usually removes quite a bit of the offending critters, so eating cooked veggies (or heavily cooked dishes) might be better, if you're at all nervous. I would also recommend that you eat as many fermented foods (sauerkraut, miso, tempeh, etc.) that you can find, as they are not only usually safer, but also have many beneficial natural probiotics within them that can help to keep your gut flora (and you) happy. When your gut flora is balanced, your immune system and digestion are optimized (among other things). If for some reason you find yourself without your bottled water and are extremely thirsty (and can't get bottled water), then you might consider some type of tea, as the water was most likely boiled to make it.

> **The best thing to do when visiting a destination with known water issues is to plan ahead and give your immune system a boost with some extra supplements.**

I always use the YL DiGize oil, enzymes (YL Essentialzyme, PRL Digest, or SP Enzycore), and PRL Betaine HCL (or SP Zypan) to give my digestive system some extra assistance at all meals. When traveling to certain countries (e.g. Mexico), I create a bottle of special capsules that I take twice a day just for extra insurance. I add the following YL essential oils into veggie caps and store them in an empty supplement bottle:

- 5 drops DiGize
- 2 drops Peppermint
- 1 drop Ginger
- 1 drop Frankincense
- 2 drops Lemon
- 1 drop Thieves

You can purchase empty vegetable caps from YL or a local health food store. Then, you open them up, add the oils above, put the other side of the cap on, and you're all set. This helps to create a special shield that will assist if something slips by – for example, having a drink with ice (frozen from the offending water). I also include probiotics daily, as they will help to keep my microbiome in balance. These are just a few precautions that I take, and then, of course, I pay close attention to the things that I'm eating.

If you are in a safe city (with regard to water), you might want to visit the local farmers market. Most cities have these events over the weekend, so if you happen to be in town, drop by to pick up some goodies for the week. If you are eating any of the fruits and veggies from the market (and are concerned), you might use some YL Lemon oil or Thieves spray to clean them off first. If you are not eating the skin (i.e. things you peel like bananas, oranges, etc.), then it might not be as big of an issue. I remember one week in Buenos Aires, where our IBM expense allowance didn't cover the cost of three meals because prices there had risen so quickly. We went to the farmers market on Sunday, and I bought a bottle of honey, some nuts and fruit, and that became the supply for my breakfast for the week.

If you are willing to go to the effort (especially for longer-term domestic trips), you might consider shipping some food and a blender ahead to your hotel. Then you'll have all of your meals ready to go. The only challenge with this can be the social aspect of eating alone. But, there are options. You could eat a healthy meal and then join your friends for dinner and eat more lightly. You can also add to your food supply by picking up a few healthy food items as you tour around the city.

Let's Go to Dinner (or Breakfast or Lunch)

Now you know from earlier in the book that I'm a big fan of spending time with people who you don't normally get to see, so having dinner with friends and co-workers after a long work day is a priority (at least for me). Some of my best memories from traveling were from meals with my co-workers or friends. Our society has become so technology dependent (with texting and social media) that it seems we rarely get to look people in the eye anymore, let alone actually talk with them. I know it might be easier to order room service and just work in your room, but please use this opportunity to get out and see the city and get to really know some of your fellow travelers.

> **My number one priority when I visit a new country is to befriend a local.**

It is *so* nice when you can find a local resident to show you around and especially to join you for meals. It really comes in handy when you don't understand the language. My experience has shown that the locals really respect you for trying to learn some of their language. At a minimum, I try to learn to say: hello, goodbye, please, and thank you, and I smile when I talk (smiling is universal!). Making the effort to speak their language really makes them smile (and sometimes laugh) and connects me instantly with them. I remember my first visit to Istanbul, where my new local friend came with me to visit the city. This was fantastic as they recommended that we "get the kebab *here* - you don't want to get the kebab *there*" . . . very nice!

When visiting foreign countries, I also observe cultural nuances, such as pace and space. Some cultures move and speak rather slowly, so it's a good idea to adapt to their norm if you can. You might also become aware of personal space, as some cultures like to stand right next to you while speaking, while others stand farther away. These points of awareness will help to reduce stress on both sides.

One of the many challenges of the business dinner is that it is typically eaten later at night, involves a lot of food, sometimes alcohol, and your next activity is usually sleep. The best way I know of to avoid over-eating is to drink a large glass of water before I head out to dinner. I take my nighttime supplements at this time.

Often times, our ravenous appetite is really a sign of dehydration.

As a general rule, it's usually better to eat dinner earlier rather than later, as your body needs at least two hours (if not more) to digest your dinner before bedtime. The body uses its sleep/rest time to do a variety of healing and cleansing activities, and you don't want to interfere with this by asking it to devote some of that energy to digesting your dinner.

As a business traveler, I'm sure you've had that night in the hotel room where you're "fighting" your dinner until three in the morning . . . no fun. The legendary travel mega-meal can be quite unpleasant . . . later on that night. At home, our family usually eats dinner around 6:00 PM or so. You can imagine the culture shock when I first visited Buenos Aires, where dinner at 10:00 PM is common! I remember going with our team to a restaurant down there at 8:00 PM and looking through the glass windows where they were just setting the tables. So, depending on the culture of your destination, you may or may not have much of a choice when it comes to dinner time. In the case of Buenos Aires, I would just eat a snack (maybe a health bar) around 6:00 PM and then try to have a lighter meal whenever we sat down for a late-night dinner. This is not easy to do, because the food down there is usually really good . . . and heavy on the meats, which can lead to some challenging nights in the hotel room as mentioned before.

Here are a couple of things to keep in mind when you're eating your dinner. The first thing you'll want to do is minimize the amount of liquids you drink with dinner. The body creates acid and enzymes to help digest food and turn it into consumable nutrition for our cells. When you drink water or other liquids with your meal, it dilutes these digestive aids and makes it more difficult for your body to digest the meal. If you do drink any liquids (hopefully filtered water), it's usually best to have it be at room temperature or warmer. I like to drink water with lemon (and no ice), as the lemon helps the lymphatic system to flush toxins, among other things. I have many friends that just drink hot water with lemon, which is excellent. It is best to squeeze the lemon into the water and not leave the lemon wedge in the cup as it might be contaminated. It is even better to use a few drops of YL Lemon oil in your water, as you will get the many health benefits of this oil, such as antibacterial support, lymphatic support, and acid/alkaline balance.

One of the biggest challenges when it comes to dinner at some restaurants is the alluring basket filled with bread. You know what I'm talking about.

There's nothing like a basket filled with the scent of hot bread wafting your way when you're starving to kick off the mega-meal. Depending on the type of bread (hot/cold, fresh/old, etc.), this can be a challenging denial. Your best choice is to just tell the waiter "no thanks," but since you're not the only one in the group (hopefully), the basket of piping hot bread is probably going to land in the middle of the table, along with a bowl of butter. Now you have to decide if it's worth it to have some. I do my best to avoid the bread unless everyone at the table is moaning with delight. If that's the case, then your next best option is to limit your intake.

One quick note here on grains. As I've suggested before, it's best to limit wheat whenever you can. There's a great book called *Wheat Belly*[10] that details how the wheat in the U.S. has been hybridized so much that it's not even close to the original "amber waves of grain" that we know and love from the song "America the Beautiful." These modifications, which may be great for growing more wheat more quickly (great for profits), are not easily digested (literally) by the body. I've heard stories of people who are severely sensitive to wheat in the U.S. but go to Europe and eat the bread and not have any reactions! Hmmm.

I really hesitate to even bring up the topic of alcoholic drinks, but we all know that drinking alcohol is just a part of most business dinners, so I'll give you my opinion. There are actually some health advocates that recommend drinking wine every day. I'm not here to debate that, but I do believe it's acceptable to have wine in moderation with your dinner companions when you travel. The biggest challenge with wine (other than the alcohol, which the liver has to deal with), is the concentration of toxins (pesticides, herbicides, etc.) introduced into the bottle from the originating grapes. It's always best if you can get an organic wine (grapes grown without the use of pesticides, fungicides, etc.) to avoid this issue, but sometimes that's not possible. I tend to favor red wine, as it has more phytonutrients (and less sugar), specifically the popular resveratrol, which is known as a very potent antioxidant. White wine is fine, but typically has more sugar content. The key here is moderation and balance. It's okay to have a glass (maybe two) of wine with dinner during your trip, but not a bottle each night.

There are some countries where wine is just part of the meal . . . period (like France or Italy). There is quite a bit of debate on this, but depending on your lifestyle, you may be able to get away with drinking a glass of wine every night (even after your trip). You have to listen to your body, as it will usually let you know if it's not happy.

The biggest challenge with other alcoholic drinks tends to be the high sugar content, especially drinks with lots of colors and little umbrellas in them. If you are drinking pure vodka, whiskey, or other alcohols straight, then you're just having to deal with the body processing the alcohol (discussed below). I know that many people prefer beer, but just realize that it comes from grains, so you have to deal with the impact of grains (e.g. pesticides, GMO, sugars, etc.) and alcohol that is present.

From a health perspective, your liver has to process the alcohol, and it's usually pretty busy trying to detox your body from your daily activities (e.g. toxins from food, air, water, etc.) and stress. The liver is amazing in its ability to detoxify the body (among the myriad other activities that it performs), but we have to be careful not to intentionally burden it, especially while we're traveling.

If you do drink a little too much, you'll want to drink as much filtered water as possible before you go to bed. Most of the unpleasant symptoms from hangovers are due to dehydration. You may have to get up to go the bathroom during the night (and I'd recommend that you drink more water when you do get up), but it's better than being hung over the next day for your business meetings. In some parts of the world, drinking is just culturally accepted, so do your best to limit your intake as you feel comfortable.

To be clear, I'm not advocating drinking alcohol as a way to stay healthy on your trip, but I am providing some suggestions to help you deal with the real world situations that will most likely occur. No one is forcing you to drink alcohol if you don't want it (even though I've had some friends in Asia that can be quite aggressive) . . . the choice of what you put into your body is always up to you.

It's usually a good idea to take some supplemental enzymes and/or PRL Betaine HCL, depending on the meal you're eating. As we get older (let's say forties plus), our bodies naturally make less HCL (hydrochloric acid) in the stomach, which is the main thing that helps to digest meat. If you are eating a big steak at dinner, you'd be well advised to take some additional acid (in the form of Betaine HCL) in the middle to the end of that meal, along with your digestive enzymes.

Food Combining

Food combining is an approach to being aware of the types of foods that we eat at the same time. The body digests different types of foods in different ways. For example, it takes the body quite a bit of time (2+ hours) and quite a bit of stomach acid to digest meat, but it digests certain vegetables (e.g. green leafy ones) more quickly and doesn't require as much stomach acid. Starches, like potatoes, are probably somewhere in the middle with regard to time and tend to absorb excess stomach acid. So, one example of a food combining principle is that you shouldn't eat meat and potatoes at the same meal.

Eat meat and potatoes separate from one another.

What? This is a basic American food staple for many, as in "I'm a meat and potatoes kind of guy." Unfortunately, eating these two things together can lead to somewhat of a digestive struggle that you'd rather not experience. Your body is producing a bunch of acid to help digest the meat, and the potatoes are absorbing the acid. So you end up with a very full/ dense feeling in your stomach, as your body will do its best to digest these things together, and you won't feel very good and may notice a drop in energy. It's much better to eat non-starchy vegetables with meat – say broccoli, carrots, or spinach. Your body will thank you later, as you head to your hotel room for a restful night of sleep.

Another key principle involves eating fruit separately.

Fruit, which typically contains a great deal of water and sugar (fructose), tends to digest very quickly, and is ideally consumed by itself. So, eat fruit first thing in the morning or for a snack, and wait at least thirty minutes before eating anything else. If you eat fruit at the end of the meal, as some cultures would have you do, you might be setting yourself up for some serious indigestion. For example, if you eat only non-starchy vegetables with your steak for dinner, and follow that up with a dessert filled with fruits, the fruit (which digests very quickly) will be stuck behind the slower digesting meat. This basically leads to the fruit fermenting in your gut, which is not pleasant. There is an exception to this, and that is pineapple. Pineapple contains bromelain, a special digestive enzyme that will actually help the pineapple get digested and provide enzymatic support to help digest other foods too. You still don't want to eat too much of this after a meal though. I would recommend that you investigate the principles of food combining, as there are many books and blogs on this topic.

Your basic guide, in terms of an eating strategy, is to eat your biggest meal at breakfast, have a smaller lunch (mid-day), and eat the least amount for dinner. Your body cycles are set up with the most digestive "power" in the morning (called *agni* by Ayurvedic doctors), so it can help to process more food then. You will find that you get your best sleep on an empty stomach, as the body won't have to expend extra energy to digest your meal while it's trying to sleep (and perform the many other maintenance duties that occur).

But, if your friends force you (just kidding) to eat a big meal for dinner, even with all of the wrong combinations, you still have some options. One of the best things you can do after dinner is go for a walk. So, if at all possible, try to walk to the restaurant (or at least walk back to the hotel after dinner).

Another huge helper is the YL DiGize oil blend. You can drink 2-4 drops of DiGize in a small glass of water at the restaurant after your meal or after you get back to your room. Some people prefer to apply it topically, so just rub a few drops directly on the skin over your stomach area. Another option is to put the drops into an empty capsule and swallow it. You'll have to experiment to see which works better for you.

The best way to avoid indigestion is by not eating too much and observing proper food combining principles.

Peppermint essential oil is also incredibly powerful as a digestive aid. You can also use the YL Peppermint internally with a few drops in a little glass of water after your meal. I don't recommend taking any other brands of essential oils internally, as you have to be careful about the quality of the essential oils. The Young Living oils are therapeutic grade and some can be taken internally. You may be thinking, "Why can't I just eat some peppermint candies from the restaurant?" Well, you could, but while good intentioned (peppermint), most of these candies contain a lot of sugar (and other ingredients) with artificial flavoring . . . not the same thing as the pure oil from which we really get relief.

Summary

○ Eat things that grow

○ Supplement with whole food products, as required

○ Limit sugar, dairy, and wheat

○ Don't miss out on the local delicacies

○ Eat cooked or fermented foods in locations with questionable water quality

○ Take specific supplements to protect you from contaminated water

○ Visit a farmers market if you can to get some extra food

○ Eat out with new friends – befriend a local

- Drink a large glass of water *before* you go to dinner

- Eat earlier, if you can

- Don't drink beverages while eating, if you can avoid it

- Limit your alcohol

- Take enzymes and possibly Betaine HCL with your meal, as required

- Observe basic food combining principles

- Eat your biggest meal at breakfast, next largest at lunch, and smallest at dinner

- Go for a walk after dinner to aid digestion

- Use special digestive support after a large meal, as required

Chapter 8

I Don't Have Time to Exercise

Traveling can be quite difficult for those of us who have a regular exercise routine. If you're traveling for a few days or a week, it's okay to break the cycle every now and then. It's kind of like stressing out over eating certain foods during the holidays (Nov-Dec). As one of my old teachers used to say: "It's not what we eat between Thanksgiving and New Year's Day – it's what we eat between New Year's Day and Thanksgiving!"

It is definitely a different story if you are training for a triathlon or some big event, as you are likely tracking all sorts of metrics daily. If that's the case, then you will have to be creative to get your workout log completed.

I'm not advocating that you sit around and eat junk food during the trip (because it's only a few days). All I'm saying is that some people stress out (and we don't want more stress) that they won't be able to get in their exercise routine while on the road, and I'm saying it's okay. Do the best you can.

> **Exercise the week before you leave and the week after you return home.**

My approach is to make it up before I leave for the trip, and upon my return. For example, I usually like to do two or three yoga and Zumba classes per week, so I might try to step that up to four or five classes the weeks before and after my trip.

I already mentioned one idea to step up your exercise during the trip, and that is to walk around the airport as much as you can before your flight. Walking is one of the best exercises around and can be your primary exercise when traveling (along with climbing stairs). As most airports are beginning to look more and more like malls, it can be tempting to stroll slowly and visit all the shops. That's okay, but I'm really suggesting that it might be more worthwhile to walk from one end of the terminal to the other at a fairly brisk pace. You can walk by all of the stores on your quick stroll, then come back and visit shops after you've walked for 15-20 minutes. If you are pulling your wheeled luggage behind you, be sure to switch hands every now and then to keep your back and arms balanced. You don't want to focus too much on only one side of your back or shoulder, as it might cause tightness and/or pain before you get on the plane. I usually have on a backpack, and will take that off and start doing mini-curls with it. I just hold it by the top handle with one hand and curl up as I'm walking. To keep things balanced, I alternate sets, switching hands.

Once you arrive at your destination airport and are walking toward the exit (or baggage claim), you may see moving sidewalks and escalators. I recommend that you avoid those in lieu of stairs and more walking to get that little extra exercise, especially after sitting on a plane for a long flight.

Another one of my favorite forms of exercise on the road is the stairs. When possible, I only use the elevator to get to my room on check-in and check-out (when I have my bags with me). After that, I like to take the stairs to my room. I say 'when possible,' because sometimes you are in a high-rise hotel, and I'm not going to trek up and down 45 flights of stairs every morning and night on my way to and from work. I have, however, been known to put on my workout clothes and run up and down the stairs just for exercise. In this case, I can usually go from my floor to the top or bottom and back. It's a great workout, but you have to be careful not to go too fast so you don't trip. Also, most hotel stairwells are not the prettiest looking or smelling places, so I'll leave this potential adventure up to you. You can also use the stairs at your workplace instead of the elevator or escalator during your trip.

> **There are opportunities to exercise all around us, if we'll just look.**

Obviously, you might want to plan your day so that you can use the hotel's exercise facilities. Some people like to get up extra early to work out or use the facility at night after dinner. I've worked with many people who like to use the elliptical machine, treadmill, weights, swimming, or attend classes. It's fine if you can work it in but, in my opinion, I'd rather spend this time seeing sights in the city or having a nice meal with people I don't normally get to see if that is an option. If you can work it all in, that's great, but most trips involve so many activities that it's hard to do it all. It's also entirely possible to do some exercise in your hotel room using internet videos for things like yoga and other types of exercise classes. Some hotels are now offering more and more services and classes to cater to healthy travelers.

Keep in mind that there are other things that you can do to support your body while on the road. While it's not exercise, activities like massage can provide huge benefits to travelers, which is one reason that you are seeing more and more of this in airports. I remember taking a long overnight flight from Rome to Beijing. Since I have a hard time sleeping on planes, I rested most of the way (suspended animation) and was a bit tired once we arrived. After getting to our hotel in Beijing, we found a foot massage spa not very far away, so we got to walk (always great after a long flight), and got a fabulous foot massage (which are usually fairly inexpensive in Asia). This was one of the best ideas we ever had, as we felt completely refreshed and ready to go afterwards. After that, this became a travel habit whenever possible after long flights. Wouldn't it be great if there were a "massage" category on your company's expense reimbursement forms?

I approach each destination as a place I'll never get to visit again, so I would rather see a few more unique sights than log an extra 45 minutes on the treadmill or elliptical rider, as I can do that at home. It's all about priorities. And while exercise is important, please consider that you may be missing out on some unique opportunities.

Along the same lines, and this can be a controversial topic, I know quite a few frequent travelers who spend the majority of their time in their hotel room doing email and/or other "work." If possible, schedule this work while you are waiting at the airport, or on the plane. I know that life/work balance can be challenging (especially these days), but it's so sad to hear stories from these folks who have been to amazing places all over the world, but "never had a chance to see anything" as they didn't leave the hotel.

This is all about priorities, but as we know today, the work world can absolutely consume us. There are some situations where you just don't have an option, but others with more soft deadlines give you a choice. I was so fortunate on many of my trips, because I was traveling with some really fun people and we would do our best to keep those on our team from spending their nights working in their hotel room (we had to be quite persuasive at times). On one particular trip in Singapore, four of us had to work pretty hard to get one of our class instructors to join us for a visit to the night zoo, a unique place to be sure. We worked on her all day, and finally got her to commit to join us. It's a longer story than I'll go into here, but let's just say that I know five people whose stomachs never hurt so much from laughing. It was truly a memorable experience, and I know she'll never regret joining us as opposed to a solo evening of responding to email. People who are on their deathbed mostly regret the things that they didn't do, and that was rarely more work.

Please take advantage of every opportunity that you can while traveling – enjoy the place and the people.

And now, back to exercise. One way to get out of the hotel and get some exercise at the same time is to walk around the neighborhood of the hotel. Please make sure that you ask the concierge or front desk personnel if and where it's safe to walk around, as you don't want to find yourself in the wrong neighborhood, especially if you're alone. If there are some unique tourist spots fairly close to the hotel, you might consider walking instead of getting a taxi. There are some great cities where you can literally walk around all day, like Rome, Buenos Aires, Amsterdam, Chicago, New York, Paris, San Francisco . . . and many more. It's an added bonus if you can find a nice park to walk around. There are also cities where it's simply not safe to walk around by yourself (or even in groups), so be sure to ask the people at the front desk before you take off.

If the weather is not very conducive to walking, or it's not safe, ask the concierge if there is a mall near the hotel. Malls are a great place to walk around – as you might get to experience some new stores

– and they are usually weather independent.

If you rented a car, you have more mobility and can visit more places. Park your car a little farther away in the parking lot just to get a little extra walking time. I always chuckle when I see people cruising the parking lot at the health club for a close spot . . . so that they can go in and exercise. I sometimes find myself doing the same thing! We are funny animals, aren't we?

Summary

○ Use walking and stair climbing as your main source of exercise – avoid elevators and escalators when possible

○ It's okay if you don't go to the gym to work out every day while traveling – do the best you can

○ Do more exercise before and after your trip to compensate for the days you don't exercise while traveling

○ Walk briskly from one end of the airport to the other – consider some arm curls with your backpack or briefcase

○ Use the hotel's health facilities, if you can fit it into your schedule

○ Exercise in your room – use internet videos or other travel exercise ideas

○ Support your body with massages – whole body or foot massages

○ Get out of the room as much as possible – unless you have no choice

○ Exercise by walking around the city and sightseeing

○ Walk around a nearby mall if the weather is not conducive to outdoor walking (or if it's not safe to walk the streets)

Chapter 9

I Don't Feel So Good . . .
Now What?

Even though we do our best to prevent illness, sometimes things just happen and we have to do our best to deal with them. This is why we spent so much time packing the "just in case" supplements before our trip. The suggestions I am giving you here are the ones that I would use if this were to happen to me.

As a natural health doctor, my focus and training are on giving people the tools that they can use to take responsibility for their lives and utilize preventive health practices using lifestyle choices, nutrition, energy healing techniques, and supplements (among other things). I have found that this type of health care is excellent at prevention and helping chronic illnesses. But, when it comes to acute care – like a car accident or some other health crisis – we are so fortunate to have the vast knowledge and experience from our medical doctors. I am simply amazed by the ability of surgeons to work their magic on people who have suffered some type of major accident. As I often tell my clients, if you break your leg, go to the emergency room and get acute care right away (and be thankful that it's there) – then call me and we can use some techniques to help your body heal more rapidly now that the crisis is over. All that to say, if you think you are really sick while traveling, then you should consult a local medical doctor *immediately.* The ideas and suggestions in this chapter are more related to the common, but very annoying, illnesses like viruses, sore throat, sinus infections, digestive issues, etc.

> **One of the keys to a natural approach to avoiding illness is that you MUST begin acting IMMEDIATELY upon your awareness that something is not right in your body.**

The more you work with this type of lifestyle, the more sensitive and attuned you become to your body, and your ability to feel the slightest imbalance becomes readily noticeable. For many people, the first sign of imbalance is a scratchy throat. For others, it could be sinus congestion, or just feeling "yucky." Once an illness (especially viruses) sets in, it's difficult for any holistic remedy to help you get rid of it quickly (i.e. in a day or two), so you really want to act as quickly as you can . . . **I can't stress this enough!**

I can't possibly talk about all of the potential health issues that you can have while traveling, but I will mention a few of the most common ones here.

General (Feel like I'm coming down with something)

As soon as I notice that I'm starting to feel a little imbalanced, I immediately do the following:

1.   I double up on my Juice Plus+ – so instead of taking 2 Fruit and 1 Vineyard capsules in the morning and 2 Veggie and 1 Vineyard capsules at night, I'll double those amounts to give my body a little extra nutritional support. We know from lots of research[11] that JP has a powerful effect on the immune system.

2.   If I have a scratchy throat, I will spray two pumps of YL Thieves Spray in my mouth a few times

throughout the day. If you packed some YL Thieves Lozenges, this would be a good time to use those as well.

3. I take one capsule of YL Inner Defense twice a day.

4. I like to chew on two or three YL Super C chewables to get an extra boost of Vitamin C. I also swallow four capsules of PRL Premier Vitamin C (or 6 tablets of SP Cataplex C), as it is a completely whole food form. The worst thing that can happen by taking too much is that you will get diarrhea, but you really have to consume quite a bit for this to happen (30+ capsules?). As with most supplements, quality is the key. I am not a huge fan of isolated, synthetic vitamins (ascorbic acid - which many people call Vitamin C). The whole food form where Vitamin C is prevalent (such as camu, acerola cherries, lemon, etc) tends to be better absorbed by the body and more effective, as you get the rich bioflavonoid co-factors as well.

5. I will put a few drops of YL Thieves oil blend on the bottom of each foot twice a day (then put on socks), and will also put a few drops on my tongue. Some people like to do this preventively, and that's fine. There is another oil blend from YL called ImmuPower that is also great to use on a daily basis on the bottoms of the feet, especially while traveling.

If for some reason you can't find your supplements, didn't pack them, or your luggage went on a trip of its own, there are still things that you can do. I would recommend that you go to the restaurant and ask them if you can please have a few cloves of garlic. If you'll open up and suck on a clove of garlic a few times per day, you'll most likely notice some improvement in your symptoms. If they don't have garlic, ask about other herbs, like clove or turmeric. After all, most of our best supplements come from these herbal sources. You're just getting it in its whole food form.

If I still notice an imbalance the next day, I'll add five capsules of SP Congaplex three or four times the next day (along with the same items above).

One of the MOST important things that you can do if you begin feeling sick is to AVOID all sugar, dairy, and wheat!

Sugar, dairy, and wheat tend to depress the immune system pretty quickly, and my purpose, once I start feeling symptoms, is to give my body extra nutritional and herbal support *and* remove things that might detract from the immune system's ability to heal my body. With that in mind, I focus heavily on eating extremely clean, and/or very lightly. What I mean by eating clean is that I try to eat *only* fruits and vegetables (which many health enthusiasts say is the way we should eat all of the time . . . can't argue with that, but it's all part of the balance).

I also drink only water, and as much of it as I can. Water helps to flush the lymphatic system, and will aid your immune system in moving things along. I take my Colloidal Silver in addition to the items above to help my body remove the pathogens that may be causing the issues. It's best to drink warm or hot water, preferably with the juice of some lemon in it (or a few drops of YL Lemon essential oil) and maybe a little honey. You might also drink some hot herbal tea. If you are traveling internationally, you might ask the locals what they recommend. Sometimes, they have a great local remedy. If not, then any form of green tea is probably a good idea.

I have to share a good story about green tea. On one of my trips to South America, I was leading a sales class (my IBM job) and asked the people at the hotel if I could have some green tea. Now, we had to go through some translation (*té verde*), but it appeared that they understood (I'm still working on my Spanish). They came back a few minutes later with a green box of tea . . . black tea. But, it was in a green box. So, I tried again and they nodded and off they went. A few minutes later they came back with another box of tea. This time the box wasn't green. I tried to read the ingredients (all in Spanish, of course) and saw that the main ingredient was senna (which is green). Having studied herbology in my doctorate courses, I knew that senna was a laxative (yikes!). I thought about the folks that may not have known that and the wonderful surprise they would get while presenting in front of the class after drinking a few cups. So, we tried again and I finally got my *té verde.*

We have a certain amount of energy in our "tank" each day, and the more of that energy that we can conserve for our immune system, the better. If I can divert the energy that my body would use to digest a large meal to the immune system, then that will help speed the healing process.

The other area where you can divert energy to your immune system is in the exercise category. I talked earlier about how you can get exercise while on the road, but now is the time for giving your body rest. Take the elevator or escalator when possible. Take a taxi to the office instead of walking. Try to squeeze in a nap in the middle of the day if at all possible. And, in general, do your best to rest and conserve energy wherever possible, so that your body can use all of that extra energy to help you heal quickly. You may even have to pass on that wonderful dinner with friends, but hopefully only for one night. When I do the above items, I find that the next day I am usually back to normal.

Allergies

Sometimes you may find yourself in an environment with some new (or familiar) pollen that results in allergy symptoms. When I get into this situation, the first thing that I'll do is use the neti pot (as described earlier) to rinse out my sinuses twice a day with the salt water. This will go a long way in helping to keep the pollen load down as much as possible. I will then take a few capsules of PRL Allercaps several times a day, as needed. It's also a good idea to take additional enzymes, as they will also help the body manage the allergic symptoms.

SP Antronex is a natural antihistamine and can do wonders for keeping your allergies in a manageable state, and you can take several tablets every few hours throughout the day. I would try to limit this to no more than 15 or so per day, though you can probably take more if needed, with little safety concerns. YL Lavender oil is also a huge antihistamine and can be taken orally and applied topically. Vitamin C is also very beneficial in managing allergies, so consider using those products as described above.

Headache

I have had times where I felt a headache coming on, and when that happens, I simply grab my bottle of YL Peppermint oil, put two drops in my palm, rub my palms together in a circle, and cup them over my nose. After taking a few deep breaths, I notice that my head feels clear. I realize that this won't always be the case for everyone, but at least give it a try.

The *Essential Oils Desk Reference,* or one of the other great books on essential oils, has a huge list of potential remedies to health issues using essential oils. I have the hardcover version of the book at home (it's pretty large), but I also purchased access to the online version for when I'm traveling. There is a pocket reference guide as well, which is very handy.

Indigestion

We talked a little about this earlier, but if I find that my stomach is upset, the first thing I do is put three or four drops of YL DiGize in a very small amount of water and drink it. You can do this every hour if needed. I can't tell you how many times this has saved me while on the road.

> **YL DiGize is one bottle of oil that you definitely want to travel with!**

If you have not been taking your probiotics, then this would be a great time to start. I would take two or three YL Life 5 probiotic capsules twice a day until I felt better.

Sometimes we'll know why our stomach is upset – overeating, that rich dessert that our friends made us eat (it's easier to blame them) or eating the wrong things. If that is the case, then DiGize will most likely do the trick. The good thing about using the oils is that even if you can't take anything orally, you can still benefit from them by applying them topically on the skin. If you just ate fruits and vegetables and ate really clean, and still feel really bad, then we might suspect some issues with the food. I would try the DiGize first, and if I didn't notice any relief in 15 minutes, I would begin taking the SP Gastrex. If I suspected food poisoning, I'd take 9-20 capsules ASAP and go to bed. If I still felt sick three hours later, I would take 6-15 additional capsules. SP Gastrex is mostly bentonite clay and will grab the toxins in the digestive tract and escort them out of the body.

High Altitude

If you've ever experienced altitude sickness, you know that it can be quite debilitating. According to WebMD.com[12], altitude sickness occurs when you cannot get enough oxygen from the air at high altitudes. This causes symptoms such as a headache, nausea, diarrhea, loss of appetite, and trouble sleeping. It happens most often when people who are not used to high altitudes go quickly from lower altitudes to 8,000 ft. (2,438 m.) or higher. For example, you may get a headache when you drive over a high mountain pass, hike to a high altitude, or arrive at a mountain resort.

The key here is that you need to check the elevation of your destination city. I remember the first time I flew to Johannesburg, South Africa and was surprised by the altitude, the — the same with Mexico City. I have found that taking SP Cataplex E2 can be very helpful in boosting your red blood cells' ability to carry more oxygen, and therefore to help reduce any symptoms of altitude sickness. I typically take six tablets daily (can either take two tablets three times per day, or three tablets twice per day) about a week before my trip (and during). I also recommend that you drink about a gallon of purified water during this time as well. We are helping to condition our blood for the higher altitude. Remember, it takes some time for your body to adjust, but we want to do our best to have our body adjust *before* we get there.

Here is a great Jin Shin Jyutsu technique to help with high altitude issues. This is a self-help posture that helps with breathing in general, and can assist the body in this case as well. You simply hold the nail bed of the ring finger with the thumb. I recommend that you do this on both hands as often as needed.

Motion Sickness

Here's another technique from Jin Shin Jyutsu that I would recommend. Hold the palm of one hand over the back of the other wrist until the feeling passes. If flying makes you anxious, hold the index finger of one hand with your other hand and breathe deeply.

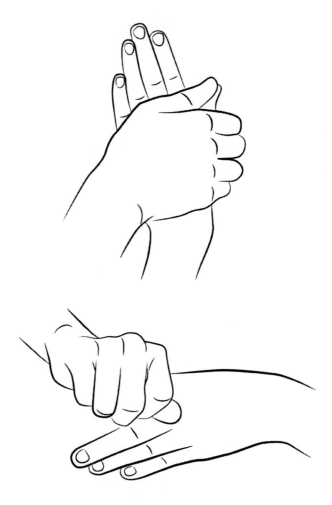

YL Ginger essential oil can be extremely helpful with motion sickness and nausea. Put a few drops in the palm of one hand, rub your palms together and hold over your nose so that you can inhale the wonderful smell. You might also put a few drops around your wrists and temples.

Overcoming Anxiety Associated with Traveling

Going to the airport and getting on a plane can be an exciting or scary event, depending on your perspective. Air travel certainly used to be a lot more fun than it is today. But, even with things like the joy and wonder of airport security, you can do your best to make this a pleasant experience. The first thing you might want to consider is any level of anxiety that you are feeling about the trip. About a week or so before a long international trip, I used to feel some anxiety, not so much about the actual flight, but more about the unknowns of the foreign country that I was about to visit. It usually showed up as an "unhappy tummy" – a little queasiness in that special intuitive area of the body around the stomach. After all, I was about to spend 10+ days in a country where they didn't really even speak English . . . and I was traveling by myself.

With that in mind, it's important to use this experience as an opportunity to help you clear some old programs (or beliefs) that might be running in your subconscious about safety, security, and letting go. You see, these programs were installed in your subconscious during childhood, and certain events can trigger them to play out. One way to think about them is like a recorder – your brain recorded the details of an event and your reaction to it, and stored it in your subconscious mind. For example, if you happened to go on a long trip as a child, and got sick on that trip, then any time you go "on a trip" as an adult that memory or recording gets triggered, and the fear and associated anxiety just appear (and sometimes the sickness too). There are many books that talk about the best ways to reprogram these brain patterns, so I won't go into details here (you might research more on Emotional Freedom Technique or EFT as one example), but I would recommend that you use this trip as a way to help you rewrite these programs once and for all. This is really important if you are a frequent traveler, as pre-trip (as well as during-trip) anxiety can be a real nuisance and may interfere with your ability to truly enjoy your travels. I have a list of recommended books, DVDs and other resources on my website at www.JohnAyo.com/favorites.

One thing that I like to do is just sit quietly, listen to my gut (where the anxiety is coming from), and ask it what I'm anxious about. I usually get some type of message when I present this question. Some of you may hear something, while others may see words or just feel a response. I usually feel the response if I'm quiet enough, and it usually has something to do with the unknowns associated with traveling by myself to a foreign country. The "what-ifs" kick in, and my brain takes over from there: What if they lose my bags? What if I get sick? What if . . . I'm sure you know what I'm talking about.

Most things that interfere with our routine will cause additional stress – especially if it involves getting on a plane and going to a different city. We also know that stress is one of the biggest factors that can interfere with our health. It lowers our immune system's ability to respond to any type of health challenges, among other things. As a general rule, anything we can do to reduce stress in our lives is going to benefit our health. This is a foundational principle of most alternative health modalities – remove or reduce the imbalances/stressors in the body, and it will heal itself. This is one of the reasons that I use L.I.F.E. System biofeedback in my private practice. The device that I use helps to reduce stressors in the body, allowing it to heal itself. The point of all of this is that it would be in your best interest to use whatever works for you to help reduce stress before your trip. Some people like to get a massage or go to a spa. If it helps you to calm down, then it's probably a good idea. Unfortunately, most of our pre-trip activities are anything but stress-reducing, so this might be an area for improvement.

Your stress reduction strategies should not end the minute you step on the plane, as we are working on keeping the body healthy and happy throughout the trip. And, as an added bonus, wouldn't it be great if we could keep these activities going all the time upon our return? The most important thing is that you choose several stress reducing strategies that work for you and make sure that you do them on a regular basis.

Visualization

One technique that I use is visualization. The way I use this is to get into a meditative or prayerful state (maybe right before you go to sleep at night or just before you get out of bed in the morning) and visualize exactly how you'd like the trip to go – no traffic to the airport, you get upgraded to first class by the airline, great food, great airplane neighbor, smooth flight, well rested when you arrive . . . you get the idea. Even more important than this visualization is to actually FEEL what all of those things would FEEL like as well as the gratitude for them happening. This puts amazing energy into action that has events happening for us way beyond our ability to explain – Just trust me on this one. Do this as many times as possible before your trip. Your bonus step, if you can do it, is to then allow and accept that whatever happens once you leave for the airport is all in exact order and working for your best good. I remember one trip where I was extremely unhappy when I found out that I got bumped from my flight to the next one that was three hours later. It was a Friday, and I was ready to get home, so this was difficult to accept. But, as I got on the later flight I noticed that my original flight had not even left yet, as the plane had mechanical difficulties. Visualization helps us to set the intention for our preference, and acceptance allows us to realize that even though things don't go as we necessarily planned them it is all working out for our better good.

Summary

○ See a doctor immediately if you feel that is necessary

○ Spring into action upon the first sign of any illness

○ Visit the hotel restaurant if you don't have your supplements and suck on a clove of garlic

○ Avoid sugar, dairy, wheat, and any other specific food challenges until you are better

○ Drink hot herbal tea

○ Rest – avoid walking, sleep a little later, take a nap

○ Consider supplements to use for digestive upset, headaches, allergy reactions

o Take additional supplements if flying to a
  high-altitude location

o Use your oils as required – nausea, digestion,
  anxiety, etc.

Chapter 10

I'm Back Home!

It is so nice to return home after a trip, especially a long one. Hopefully your luggage returned home with you and you didn't bring any unwanted guests (e.g. parasites) with you. If you followed many of the suggestions set forth in this book, then you should be feeling great. In this chapter we'll talk about some ideas that might be worthwhile for you to consider now that you are back home, so that you'll remain healthy and happy and ready to travel again.

The first thing that I do when I land back home is say a prayer of gratitude for the safe and joyful completion of my trip. We are so fortunate to be able to get on a plane and travel halfway around this amazing planet in a day. It wasn't that long ago when something like that would be completely impossible. Most of our ancestors never had the option of this luxury. As with so many things in life, we tend to take safe trips for granted. I'm glad that we have such a good safety record, but there are a lot of things that can go wrong, so just a quick thought of gratitude can create an environment of peace for future journeys.

If you were on a long flight, consider some of the ideas that we discussed in the chapter about arriving at your hotel – like rinsing out your sinuses with the neti pot. It's always good to get the final remains of that airplane air (and anything else that was in it) out of your body. Also, if you traveled through several time zones to get home, don't forget to follow the recommendations from the chapter on jet lag – the most important of which is to stay awake until 9:00 PM.

As I begin to unpack, I have my updated packing list handy so that I can make any changes based on things I might have forgotten to bring. This is also the time I make a note of any replacement items that I used on the trip, so that I can order more now. It makes traveling easier for the next trip.

If you travel quite a bit, you might consider keeping duplicates of certain items already in your luggage – like toothpaste, toothbrush, supplements, travel umbrellas, etc. I like to keep a quart-size plastic bag with my carry-on items ready to go. It just makes packing the next time that much easier.

When I unpack, I put all of my clothes in a separate location (preferably not the carpet) in case there are some unwanted guests (e.g. bed bugs) on board. I try to wash these clothes as quickly as possible and add a capful of YL Thieves Household Cleaner concentrate to the clothes washer just in case. I recommend that you wash all of the clothes that you brought with you on the trip, whether you wore them or not. Being the ever efficient engineer, I have a personal challenge to pack as lightly as possible and wear everything I bring with me. For those of you who are fortunate enough to be married to an engineer, you know what a joy we can be to live with at times. I won't even go into the "correct" way to load a dishwasher.

I will continue taking all of my preventive supplements for another week or so, just to give my immune system the extra support it needs to balance out any remaining challenges from the trip. I know that many of us jump right back into our routines as soon as we get back home. If you are on a fairly short domestic trip, this might be okay. I know that I've gone from the airport back to my home office (morning flight) to get work done that afternoon. But, if you've been on a longer trip (especially international and covering multiple time zones), please give your body the rest that it needs before jumping right back into your daily routine. I know that this is sometimes not possible, but if you can, sleep a little more and take a nap or two so that your body can recover from the additional stress that it endured from the trip.

Our bodies are absolutely amazing healing machines, and sometimes we won't even feel the side effects of everything that's going on, but rest assured that your body is working hard to keep you well and going . . . give it a little break upon your return, if you can. A massage or visit to the spa might be a great idea. I am so fortunate to have an amazing spa in Dallas that I visit monthly to help keep me balanced and happy.

After you are back into your routine, don't forget about the exercise "deal" that we made before. If you didn't get a chance to exercise very much on your trip, now is the time to move into action to make up for it.

You're Home Until Your Next Trip – Now What?

I'd like to offer you some ideas on things that you can do to maintain your health in between your travels. Depending on how you were led to read this book, the following may or may not apply to you. If you just wanted some assistance on your travels, then you're done. If you would like some insight into alternative options to consider for restoring and maintaining your health on a regular basis, then read on.

I believe that one of the best things that you can do to help your body rebalance itself is a detox program called the "21-Day Purification Program" from Standard Process. The program helps your body to remove the accumulated toxins that have built up over the years (and from your travels). It provides a way to assist the organs (liver, kidneys, colon, etc.) to release the chemicals that have been stored there, along with some of the fat (toxins are known to be stored in fat). There is a Toxicity Survey on my website[13] that you can use to help you assess where you are in terms of toxic load (you would fill it out before and after the program), and it will also help you better understand the benefits gained after the 21 days. I have used this program with many clients to help them with a variety of health challenges (e.g. physical symptoms, weight loss, sleep issues, etc.) with tremendous success. You are basically taking whole food supplements several times a day along with whole-food-based shakes. There is a defined protocol and eating plan that accompanies these supplements. You can read more about the details on my website (www.JohnAyo.com) and purchase a kit there as well.

We are meant to be healthy, and there are so many things that we can do to get and stay healthy. The first, of which, is to put ourselves in a beneficial energetic space.

We are energy beings.

If the energetics of your living space is pulling energy from you, then there is that much less energy available for your body to not only keep you healthy but, more importantly, to help you thrive. The amazing technologies that are available today allow us to have so many great conveniences that were not previously available, but unfortunately these come with some cost. While it's handy to have WiFi (wireless internet) available for our cell phones and tablets, these waves from the electromagnetic spectrum tend not to be that biocompatible (meaning that it can interfere with our body's cell-to-cell communication) with our body. The 60 Hz wiring in U.S. buildings has been shown to be unhealthy as well. The wireless cell phone network, while very handy, has some implication for our health, especially when we are holding a device up against our head (inches from the brain), or wearing a smart phone on our belt. This can be even more challenging for young children who are still developing.

There are technologies that can remediate (make the waves more compatible with the body – i.e. biocompatible) these electronic devices, and I would ask you to look into those. I use the cell phone remediation tool from PRL (called Q Disc) that you can read about on my website for my smartphone. There are other good ones out there, but you have to test (using muscle testing is one way) to see which works best for you.

I highly recommend using the pyramid that we talked about for your hotel room, to remediate your bedroom or office or other room where you spend the bulk of your time back home. The small PRL Pyrafire pyramid is helpful to remediate the energetics (EMFs and other energetics) in a car or room, but you might want to look into the larger one for your home or office, as there may be other factors involved (e.g. smart meters, routers, etc.). This remediation technology for phones and buildings is constantly changing, so check my website[14] for the latest updates.

I know that some of these topics are controversial, so you might want to do a little research on your own. I have been studying these energetic topics since 1976, with a focus on the body starting in the 1990s. The only way to discern truth is to listen to your intuition (along with a little logic/thinking), and it can sometimes be quite challenging. As you'll hear from many who have walked this path, you have to follow the money to get to some answers. Let me explain.

I have seen "studies" reported on the mainstream

news that say that cell phones are completely healthy, only to find out (after some digging) that the study was funded through the back door by companies or organizations that profit from this technology. I found similar patterns around GMOs (genetically modified organisms) and vaccines. You have to do your own research to come up with your own answers. Don't just take the mainstream media news stories at face value – somebody is paying for those commercials that are around the news shows.

There are so many wonderful natural health practitioners around the world, and I would ask you to consider giving them a try. You can research these modalities and the practitioners on the Internet. Go to your local health food store and ask around, or pick up the free magazines that are present in most of them. These are great sources of information to help you find people who will comprise your health team. I am a big believer in having a health team of consultants that I can turn to for support, treatments, and consultation. You are responsible for your health, but you can enlist support from as large a team of knowledgeable practitioners as you like (medical doctors, chiropractors, naturopaths, acupuncturists, and nutritionists, to name a few).

I personally use biofeedback in my naturopathic practice (along with nutritional supplementation and essential oils) and am obviously a huge fan of this particular modality. When I was really sick, I went to several chiropractors that used similar technology and nutritional supplementation.

I am fascinated with technology and computers. As an engineer and IBMer, I was intrigued by the ability to use computers to "talk" to the body. Since everything is energy and has a signature frequency, we should be able to reproduce that frequency using a computer. If viruses, bacteria, and even emotions have unique frequencies, then why can't we use technology that is similar to noise-canceling headphones to balance those frequencies and help the body heal more quickly? This is how unconscious biofeedback works. The technology helps to balance stressors in the body, and that allows the immune system to work more effectively.

In Conclusion

Thank you for taking the time to focus on and take responsibility for your health. As each of us does the necessary work of becoming the best that we can be – mind, body, and spirit – we help to make this planet a better place for all of us. When you have your health, anything is possible. If you don't have your health, nothing else matters. I lived this and know for certain that it's true.

There is an old proverb that I used to have on my business cards – "Health is the crown on the well man's head, but only the sick man can see it." As with so many things in our life, we truly don't appreciate something until we've lost it. I am thankful each day of my life for my good health and will NEVER take it for granted again. I hope that each of you will do the same, so that you will have the opportunity to provide your gifts to this world and become the best that you can be.

Safe travels!

Summary

○ Be thankful for a safe trip and return home

○ Treat your arrival home similar to your arrival at the hotel

○ Update your packing list as you unpack

○ Continue taking your supplements as your body recovers from the trip

○ Give your body a little extra rest and pampering

○ Add extra exercise to make up for any lack during your trip

○ Schedule an appointment with your favorite natural health practitioner to maintain your health

Appendix

Sample Travel Packing Checklist

☐ **YL Essential Oils**

- ○ Thieves: waterless hand purifier, oil and spray

- ○ Valor, Peace and Calming, ImmuPower, Lemon, Peppermint, StressAway, DiGize, White Angelica, Gratitude, Lavender

- ○ Travel diffuser (plug in) or cotton balls

- ○ YL NingXia Red packets

- ○ Lip balm

☐ **Food**

- ○ Snacks

- ○ Trail mix

- ○ Energy bars – JP, SP, or YL all have good ones

- ○ Instant Oatmeal/utensils

- ○ Tea bags

□ **Electronics**

- ○ Headphones (w/extra battery)

- ○ Movies on tablet

- ○ Laptop and tablet AC adapter

- ○ International electric adapters

- ○ Smartphone power adapter (AC and DC) and extra battery

□ **Supplements**

- ○ **No Jet Lag** (homeopathic)

- ○ SP St John's Wort, Probiotics, SP Cod Liver Oil or YL OmegaGize capsules

- ○ Digestive Support – Enzymes (HCL)

- ○ Purification spray (you can use an empty Thieves bottle with 8 drops Purification and water)

- ○ PRL Melatonin

- ○ SP Cataplex E2 (for high altitude)

- ○ Eye drops

- ○ Allergy – Vitamin C, PRL Allercaps, or SP Allerplex, Neti pot, salt, Lavender, SP Antronex

- ○ Immune – Congaplex, Immuplex, Colloidal Silver, Olive Leaf Extract

- ○ Gastrex

- ○ Green Tea ND

☐ **YL soap/shampoo/conditioner**

☐ **Reading glasses**

☐ **Sunglasses**

☐ **Wash cloth** (Note: Many European countries do not have these in their hotel rooms, so it's a good idea to bring a few just in case if you use them.)

☐ **PRL PyraFire Pyramid**

☐ **Books/Kindle (power adapter)**

☐ **Passport**

☐ **Umbrella**

☐ **Baseball cap**

☐ **Jacket**

☐ **Winter**

- ○ Long underwear

○ Scarf

○ Stocking cap

○ Sleep socks

You can download this Sample Packing Checklist as a file that you can customize at the "My Favorites" page of my website: http://johnayo.com/favorites.

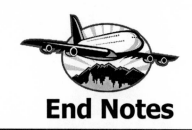

End Notes

[1] For YL Products go to http://www.michelleayo.com
For JP Products go to http://www.ayo.juiceplus.com/

[2] Peanuts article http://www.drweil.com/drw/u/id/QA A 115491

[3] *Essential Oils Desk Reference* from http://www. lifesciencepublishers.com

[4] No Jet Lag homeopathic remedy http://www.nojetlag. com/

[5] Emotional Freedom Technique (EFT) - http://www. emofree.com/

[6] Jin Shin Jyutsu https://www.jsjinc.net/

[7] PRL Pyrafire pyramid for home/office remediation of EMF http://johnayo.com/emf

[8] More Juice Plus+ info http://www.ayo.juiceplus.com/

[9] I list some of my favorite books about diet and other health topics at http://johnayo.com/favorites

[10] Check out the book *Wheat Belly* at http://johnayo.com/favorites

[11] Research for JP's powerful effect on the immune system can be found at http://www.ayo.juiceplus.com/

[12] WebMD.com http://www.webmd.com/a-to-z-guides/altitude-sickness-topic-overview

[13] Toxicity Survey to assess toxic load in your body http://www.johnayo.com/21day

[14] My websites: http://www.johnayo.com/ and http://www.travelbalance.net

CPSIA information can be obtained at www.ICGtesting.com
Printed in the USA
LVOW12s1031251114

415260LV00001B/1/P